STILL CRAZY ABOUT THE CATS

by

Jamie H. Vaught

McClanahan
Publishing House

All book order correspondence should be addressed to:
McClanahan Publishing House, Inc.
P. O. Box 100
Kuttawa, KY 42055
(502) 388-9388
1-800-544-6959

TABLE OF CONTENTS

Acknowledgments   4

1 Celtic Cat (Frank Ramsey)   7

2 Rupp Runt (Larry Conley)   24

3 Golden Boy (Cotton Nash)   42

4 Wildcat Minister (Larry Pursiful)   55

5 Big Jim (Jim Andrews)   66

6 "Oh Honey, Your Hair Is Too Long...." (Doug Flynn)   83

7 Dunk Slammer (James Lee)   102

8 Knoxville Kid (Chris Gettelfinger)   116

9 From Harlan to Lexington (Dick Parsons)   127

10 Masterful Cat (Jim Master)   161

11 Sir Winston (Winston Bennett)   177

12 Hoops Pioneer (Bernadette Locke-Mattox)   192

13 Chief Cat (C.M. Newton)   206

14 Unforgettable Cat (John Pelphrey)   239

ACKNOWLEDGMENTS

I would like to acknowledge this basketball book —
Still Crazy About The Cats — wouldn't have been possible
without the cooperation of the players or coaches who
have ties with the University of Kentucky's roundball program. The well-known individuals featured in the book
gladly took time out from their busy schedule to give their
lengthy interviews. Specifically, I would like to thank UK
athletic director C. M. Newton, a busy man, for giving me
a lot of time for the book. For that, I will always be grateful to coach Newton. There are many other former players whom I did not discuss because of space limitations or
time conflicts. They are, in no way, less entertaining or
important than the ones profiled in the book. The UK
program is so big that anyone can write several volumes
about the former stars.

The book has been a fun, but very time-consuming
project for me. The individuals who were interviewed provided many intriguing stories and comments that a hoops
junkie or a Wildcat fan would love to read. Patterned after
my 1991 book, titled *Crazy About The Cats: From Rupp to
Pitino*, which included exclusive interviews with Joe B.
Hall and Rick Pitino, this new volume is another look at
UK's tradition-rich basketball program through the eyes
of hoops personalities who have connections with the
school.

In the early stages of this book, I had plans to pro-
file the other basketball celebrities such as Ray Mears of
Tennessee and Denny Crum of Louisville, two of the
Wildcats' nemeses of the past and present. Even rival
coaches Bobby Knight of Indiana and Dale Brown of LSU
were the other possibilities. But I eventually scratched
the idea and decided to concentrate on the Wildcat individuals.

Many helpful individuals have contributed in one
way or another for this book. I would like to thank the

transcribers, including Norma Maiden and Bronwyn Marsee, for their long hours. Thanks also go to two award-winning photographers in Kentucky — Chris Jones of Harlan and David Rogers of Somerset — for contributing outstanding photos to the book. Public relations people — Tim Hix of the University of Georgia, R. Jeffrey Twiss of the Boston Celtics and Joyce Baxter of UK — were kind enough to provide photos. I also thank manager Don Brake of The Camera Shop in Somerset for printing several photographs.

Special thanks go to sports editor Neill Morgan of *The Daily News* in Middlesboro as well as my colleagues/friends at UK's Southeast Community College — Joe Marcum, Astor Simpson, Dr. Rhonda England, Chalk Stapleton and Sha Li Zhang. Anna Berry of Lexington was also helpful. The old and recent media guides from various schools, including Kentucky, were also valuable in verifying the facts and scores.

But the two books that I have written about UK would have never appeared if I hadn't shown interest in the Wildcats at a very young age. My first real experience with the Wildcats took place in March of 1966 when I was 10 years old. My brother-in-law (now deceased), a former high school coach who was about 20 years older than me, and a friend had taken me to Lexington to see UK play Tulane. It was the year of the famous Rupp's Runts squad. We had good seats — about 15 rows from the floor. While the UK freshman team played a preliminary game, I recognized four Wildcat varsity players — Pat Riley, Louie Dampier, Tom Kron and Tommy Porter — sitting in the stands. I brought my game program and politely asked for their autographs. They obliged and Kentucky eventually won the regular season finale, whipping the Green Wave by a score of 103-74.

Occasionally, my parents and I would get the unclaimed student tickets at Memorial Coliseum just a few hours before the tipoff. We saw several games in person. I can remember coach Adolph Rupp sat on the bench before a conference game with Mississippi State as he watched Dan Issel and the rest of the players warm up. Growing up in a very small rural town called Science Hill in Pulaski County, I can recall that on many school nights I excitedly watched Kentucky on delayed black-and-white telecasts which ran past one or two in the morning. I had my pajamas on and drank hot chocolate to keep me warm on wintry nights. My parents, who usually watched the games with me, worried about my lack of sleep for next day's school work, but they let me stay up late.

Well, before concluding, I would like to acknowledge my wife, Deanna, and my mother, Betty, for their never-ending support and encouragement for the second book. Needless to say, my life would've been more difficult without them. And I hope I haven't omitted any other persons who helped with this project. If I did, special thanks go to them as well.

Enjoy the book!

Jamie H. Vaught
August 1995

Celtic Cat

FRANK RAMSEY

At the end of every summer, many of his patrons at the bank are inquiring about hard-to-get tickets for Kentucky roundball games for the upcoming season.

And former Wildcat star Frank Ramsey tries to meet their requests. He is the president of Dixon Bank in rural Webster County in western Kentucky. The bank is about 20 miles north of Madisonville, also the home of a recent UK playmaker, Travis Ford.

"Everyone down here is a UK fan," said the 64-year-old Ramsey in his office. "Our customers watch it on TV, even stay up and watch the delayed telecast. They listen to it and we have season tickets for the UK basketball games and they start asking to be put on the list as early as September. Practically all of our customers are UK fans.

"They discuss the game but they are very seldom critical of UK or the coaches. They all discuss strategy. They're very knowledgeable. The TV announcers will say they (the Wildcats) should have done this and that. The fans critique every game the next day."

There aren't very many individuals who have played for two of the most fascinating and famous figures in basketball history.

Ramsey is one of the fortunate people who had the opportunity to play for the late Adolph Rupp in college and the cigar-smoking coach Red Auerbach in the National Basketball Association. For a long time, both Rupp and Auerbach were the winningest coaches of all time in collegiate and professional ranks, respectively.

Rupp currently is the winningest coach in college basketball history with 876 victories, although runner-up Dean Smith of North Carolina is closing in.

But Auerbach saw his NBA career coaching mark of 938 wins broken during the 1994-95 campaign, when Atlanta's Lenny Wilkens topped the all-time record with a victory over the Washington Bullets. After the game, Wilkens, a non-smoker who had established the record on his fourth try, lit a cigar in a fitting tribute to Auerbach. Currently, Auerbach is president of the Boston Celtics.

During the Korean Conflict of the early 1950s, Ramsey played at Kentucky where he was a two-time All-American under the watchful eyes of Rupp. Then he was selected by Auerbach of Boston in the first round of the NBA draft and became the most prominent sixth man in the league.

Ramsey not only won a national championship in 1951 and three SEC crowns while at UK, but he helped Boston win seven NBA titles during his nine-year pro career.

Ramsey said both of his coaches were somewhat similar.

"They were both dictators," he said. "They were each dealing with a different-age individual and a different type of individual. Their coaching personalities were not identical but were very similar. Coach Rupp got you straight out of high school and you did exactly what he dictated you would do. You did everything his way.

"Red was dealing with mature men with families and you would discuss what needed to be done but you knew that he had the final say in the end. He was extremely easy to play for. He demanded the best. He wanted you to be in shape. He chose people to fit in his system. Everybody who played with me while I was at Boston was drafted by Red. The player was chosen by Red to fit a specific need on the team. He chose people who came from winning programs. He did a thorough background check on their attitudes. He was smart."

While at Kentucky, Ramsey didn't lose very many games. During the Ramsey years, the Wildcats posted an unbelievable mark of 86-5, winning nearly 95 percent of the games.

But his first year in the NBA (1954-55) wasn't all that rosy. The Celtics finished with a .500 record at 36-36, which was good for third place in the Eastern Division.

"Losing was a most difficult thing to adjust to," Ramsey said. "We hadn't lost a game (at Kentucky with a 25-0 mark) the year before. We played the same type of ball that we played at UK. It was a fast-break game. It was extremely easy to fit in with the group. We didn't have any crowds in the gym at that time. Out in Rochester (where the current Sacramento Kings franchise once played), we played in a skating rink once. But I had no trouble at all."

The 6-3 Ramsey averaged 11.2 points a game as a NBA rookie. His well-known teammates include a pair of All-NBA guards Bob Cousy and Bill Sharman. Boston also had a couple of ex-UK players in 6-5 Robert Brannum (who later transferred to Michigan State from Kentucky) and 6-1 Lucian Whitaker on that squad.

One of Ramsey's teammates at Kentucky, Cliff Hagan, didn't play in the NBA at that time. He was serving in the Air Force. The 6-4 Hagan began his pro career with the St. Louis (now Atlanta) Hawks in 1956.

Later, on the hardwood floor, Ramsey played against Hagan, a rising star who would appear in five NBA All-Star Games during his pro career. "Cliff Hagan was my former roommate and at that time the big rivalry was St. Louis and Boston, and I had to guard him," Ramsey smiled. "We'd have dinner prior to or after the game. We'd kick, fight, push and then go out and have a sandwich after the game. We didn't get mad. If you get mad, you really hurt yourself."

During Ramsey's years at Boston from 1954 to '64, the Celtics and the Hawks, interestingly, met four times in the NBA Finals with Boston winning three of them.

Ramsey's best year as a pro was 1957-58 when he poured in an average of 16.5 points in guiding Boston to a NBA-best 49-23 mark. But the Celtics dropped to St. Louis, led by the league's third-leading scorer Bob Pettit, in the championship series in six games.

During the 1962-63 season, the NBA champion Celtics had eight future Hall of Fame players on the roster, including Ramsey, Sam Jones, Tom Heinsohn, Bill Russell, Bob Cousy, Clyde Lovellette, K. C. Jones and John Havlicek. In addition, they also had a would-be Hall of Famer in coach Auerbach.

In his nine pro seasons, Ramsey scored 8,378 points for an average of 13.4 points.

Ramsey retired from NBA in 1964 and entered private business in Madisonville. Later, he also did some work as a TV commentator on regional SEC telecasts.

Ramsey will never forget his first pro agreement in the summer of 1954 when he signed a basketball contract with the Celtics at a baseball stadium in Boston. Yes, the famed Fenway Park, where the Boston Red Sox play.

No, Ramsey wasn't at Fenway Park just to watch baseball. As a member of a college all-star team, he was there to play basketball outside on a portable floor in an exhibition game against the Harlem Globetrotters.

Auerbach saw Ramsey and called him over to the dugout. They negotiated for the player's contract. The Boston coach first offered him a salary of over $6,000. Ramsey said no. They eventually agreed on $8,000 and the former UK player signed his first pro contract at the park.

"We were sitting there talking," Ramsey said. "I had to go to the Army. I had a two-year obligation to the Army and he (Auerbach) wanted me to try to get a deferment and play one year. I said, 'I'd try.' We hit on a salary. That's the last time I ever talked salary with anybody.

"(Later on in his pro career) when I got ready to leave in the spring to come back to Kentucky, I'd sign a blank contract and leave it in the secretary's desk. When (then-owner) Walter Brown got around to figuring my salary, he'd fill it in and send it to me. I had no idea. We didn't have agents so we didn't talk (much in negotiating). I just took whatever they gave me. In fact, I played one year without a contract — I'd been in the Army and never signed one. Once you shook hands with him (Brown), that was it."

Unlike today's astronomical salaries earned by the NBA players, Ramsey said "the most I ever made was $20,000 (a season) my last two years of playing. I don't wish I was playing today. What we did back then is now a part of history. We won seven NBA championships and I had no idea what anybody else was making. Really, I didn't care and everybody else was there to win. Red insisted your salary did not depend on stats. It depended on whether the team won or lost. We had great teams. I am not envious of the salaries they are making (now)."

The late Earl Strom was one of the most flamboyant officials ever in the NBA. But Ramsey respected him. Like Ramsey, Strom is a Hall of Famer.

"You'd have conversations with him," Ramsey recalled. "When I was playing, it was whispering time. If you went by and said something to him, he'd say 'That will cost you $15.' You got along with him. We traveled together. There were not that many of them (officials as the league only had nine clubs). We were friends with them. You respected them. You knew if you were on the other team's homecourt, the crowd wouldn't influence them. There were only two officials (for each game). We played in some games where there was only one. He (Strom) was a great official."

Since 1958, Strom had officiated in both the NBA and the ABA before retiring several years ago.

In the 1980s, former NBA superstar Larry Bird and his Boston Celtics drew sellout crowds of nearly 15,000 in the old Boston Garden.

But in the earlier days, it was a different story. The Garden, built in 1928, did not have large turnouts when Ramsey played.

"At that time, all of the fans were hockey fans," Ramsey said. "We probably averaged 4,000 or 5,000 a game and it (Boston Garden) held 13,999. It has since converted from hockey to a basketball town. It was not a basketball town at that time. I go back to Boston quite often. I don't see them (Celtics) play. I stay in touch with all of my Boston teammates. I have a daughter (Cynthia) who lives in New Hampshire. I do go back two or three times a year."

Actually, for the record, the Celtics' average attendance at home hovered at the 7,000-8,000 mark in the late 1950s and early 1960s.

Although he was born and raised in western Kentucky, Ramsey enjoyed his stay in Massachusetts during the roundball season.

"If I had not been able to come back to Kentucky to do some businesses, I would have probably stayed there," Ramsey said. "We lived in an area — near Wellesley College — called Wellesley Hills. I enjoyed the people out there. They were almost like Kentuckians. The first year or two, they were very standoffish. Once they got to know you, they couldn't do enough for you. Like when I'd be gone on a road trip, the neighbors would invite my wife, Jean, to Christmas dinner or Thanksgiving dinner. They would stop by to check on her. Well, they were almost like Kentuckians, who are leary of strangers. But once they get to know you, then you're one of them. And they can't do enough for you."

In 1990, you may recall that it was all-female Wellesley College where former first ladies Barbara Bush and Raisa Gorbachev (of the former Soviet Union) spoke at the school's graduation exercises. First lady Hillary Clinton is also a graduate of that college where she was the student government president her senior year.

Before coming to UK in 1949, Ramsey starred at Madisonville High School. And he led his high school to a couple of state tournament appearances at the Armory in Louisville. Ramsey recalled that Rupp didn't have to recruit him because the youngster had already known about the UK campus while visiting friends who were freshmen at the university.

"When they (the coaching staff) offered me a scholarship, I jumped at it," he said. "They called my parents and the first opportunity I had to sign, I grabbed it and signed, hoping they would not take it away from me. I wanted to go there and didn't think I would play much, until maybe I was a senior, but things turned out differently. It all worked out well."

Legendary coach Ed Diddle of Western Kentucky also wanted Ramsey. The youngster was very interested but decided on Kentucky.

Asked what was the most memorable talk he had with Rupp, Ramsey replied, "There were so many of them. I remember that he would tell you that you could do something when you didn't think that it was possible. Playing at UK was like taking a class from a nobel laureate in chemistry. He instilled confidence in you. He was a great coach. UK gave me an education not only in academics but the education that I got on the floor allowed me to start out a career in basketball."

At that time, UK freshmen did not perform on the varsity level. So Ramsey first played on the freshman team, which was coached by Rupp's long-time aide, Harry Lancaster. The Kittens, led by Ramsey and Cliff Hagan, practically beat everyone as they raced to a 15-1 mark.

After the Wildcats played in the 2,800-seat Alumni Gym from 1924 to 1950, they moved to a new $4 million facility which held about four times more people than the old gym. The new 11,500-seat arena was named Memorial Coliseum in honor of the 10,000 Kentuckians who had died in World War II and the Korean Conflict.

Ramsey remembers the first game at the coliseum when he was a dark blond-haired sophomore guard. That was in December of 1950 and the matchup saw the Cats roll past a hapless West Texas State squad in a 73-43 verdict. Interestingly, that game wasn't even a sellout.

"I was scared to death," he said. "At that time, it was the largest arena in the South and you were playing for the greatest coach in the country. I was scared all the time that I would be on the team that would lose the first home game at (the coliseum). That motivated a lot of us. Your mouth was always dry like you had cotton in it. You'd get your second wind once the game started and everything just worked out."

And Kentucky went on to win 307 more home

games until 1976 when it moved to Rupp Arena. UK's all-time record at Memorial Coliseum was 308-38 for an astonishing winning percentage of 89.0.

Despite Kentucky's tradition-rich basketball history, only a handful of UK players (Wah Wah Jones, Alex Groza, Ralph Beard, Dale Barnstable, Cliff Barker, among others, from the 1948 and '49 squads) have won the national championships more than once.

Ramsey could have been a member of this elite group. He nearly won it twice. In 1951, Ramsey and the Wildcats captured the NCAA title as 7-0 center Bill Spivey poured in 22 points in a 68-58 victory over Kansas State. And in Ramsey's last year at UK (1953-54), the top-ranked Wildcats went undefeated the entire season even though ailing Rupp had heart and eye problems. They were led by the "Big Three" seniors in Ramsey, Cliff Hagan and Lou Tsioropoulos. No Wildcat team has gone unbeaten since then.

But Rupp, despite his team's glossy 25-0 mark and No. 1 ranking, refused to let his Wildcats participate in the NCAA tournament because the NCAA had ruled the "Big Three" ineligible. The players were graduate students, NCAA reasoned.

In a 1977 interview, Hagan told the author, "We were a big part of that team — the three of us. Coach Rupp did not want to go to the NCAA without us playing so Kentucky declined the invitation. That always bothered me a little bit and it bothers me more now than it did then because we placed such a great effort in getting our student-athletes to get a degree while they're at school. We didn't know that those were the rules of the game. It was too late when we discovered that the rules said if you enter graduate school, you can't participate in the NCAA championship."

One of the individual highlights of that season was Hagan's record-breaking 51-point performance against Temple in the season opener. With the help of Ramsey's passing game, Hagan established school and SEC scoring records. (In 1970, Dan Issel shattered a single-game school record held by Hagan when he pumped in 53 points against Ole Miss in Oxford.)

In the previous year (1952-53), the Wildcats did not play a regular schedule. NCAA had suspended UK for one season for various rules violations. "It was disappointing," Ramsey said of the suspension. "It was probably the best thing that happened to us because we only had six people on scholarship that year. Everybody else had graduated or transferred. We probably couldn't have beaten anybody the year I sat out; they brought in about 10 freshmen who were great players. We practiced for one whole year.

"As a student, you took your hard subjects because we practiced maybe two or three days a week. I was a normal student. We weren't playing basketball, but we had some exhibition games. The following year nobody touched us — we were undefeated."

Yes, Ramsey is widely-known for his feats in basketball, but he also played baseball for coach Harry Lancaster at UK. He was a good one, too. The outfielder was named first-team All-SEC three times (1951, '52 and '53).

One of Ramsey's close friends at UK, Hagan would later become athletic director at Kentucky. Both hailed from western Kentucky. Both had played against each other in the state tournament with Hagan from Owensboro High. So they had some things in common.

As roommates, they sometimes argued about the room temperature. Ramsey liked it cool, while Hagan wanted to stay warm. "I liked the window open with the heat (turned) off and I slept next to the window. Cliff liked the window closed and the heat on," Ramsey smiled. "Whoever went to bed first would fix it like he wanted it and whoever went to bed next fixed it the way he wanted it. If you got up during the night to go to the bathroom or something, it was changing all the time. We had one of those old steam radiators. That was just the way it was."

After five years at UK, they went separate ways with their careers and families. But they continued to stay in touch. Ramsey and his wife even named one of their two sons, Cliff, after Hagan. (Their other son, Tripp, was a student assistant coach for UK's 1978 NCAA championship team.)

One unpleasant time for Hagan took place in November of 1988. Under pressure from the UK administration, Hagan had resigned from his athletic director post during the NCAA investigation of the school's basketball program. Hagan had been serving as AD since 1975.

"I felt like he had to take the rap for everything that happened there," said Ramsey, who once served on the UK Board of Trustees. "Nobody else left (immediately). I think he has been hurt. We don't discuss it. We talk about children, grandchildren, things like that."

A few years later, the UK Board of Trustees, acting on a recommendation from athletic director C. M. Newton, renamed its newly-remodeled baseball park on campus in honor of Hagan. "I thought it was wonderful," Ramsey said. "He deserved it. He did a lot of good things for UK. (It's) a well-deserved honor."

In the fall of 1970, Ramsey returned to pro basketball after a six-year hiatus. No, he didn't go back to Boston or the NBA. He went to the Louisville-based Kentucky Colonels of the now-defunct American Basketball Association where he was hired to coach the team. While aging Rupp, nearing retirement, was still coaching the Wildcats in Lexington — one hour away from Louisville on Interstate 64, the Colonels lured Ramsey, then 39 years old, away from his successful business career in Madisonville.

Shortly after Colonels President Mike Storen announced the appointment of Ramsey as the new floor boss of the Colonels, many of Ramsey's basketball friends sent telegrams. Sending congratulations were several big-name folks like Rupp, Red Auerbach, Bill Sharman and Cliff Hagan (who had just retired from ABA's Dallas Chaparrals as player-coach).

"A guy that I had known for some time, Mike Storen, contacted me," Ramsey said. "He said that he was going to make a coaching change. I had just sold a business in Madisonville and I had some spare time. But I told him that I wasn't interested. He asked me again and I said no. Finally, he said why don't you give it a try so I did. That year we went to the finals of the ABA (against the Utah Stars, coached by Sharman, a former Celtics teammate of Ramsey's)."

Before Ramsey took the job, the Colonels were already 17 games into the season. The team was doing all right with a 12-5 mark. But Storen and popular coach Gene Rhodes reportedly had a personality conflict and Rhodes was dismissed after 15 games. Former UK All-American and Colonels business manager Alex Groza took over the coaching duties for a couple of games on an interim basis.

Ramsey's coaching record in the 1970-71 regular season wasn't spectacular. He compiled a 32-35 mark. But his team bounced back and did well in the playoffs, winning the first two rounds against the Floridians (from Miami) and a strong Virginia Squires club before losing to Utah in seven games in the championship series.

One of the highlights of the Colonels' season featured former UK All-American Dan Issel's blazing success as a pro rookie. Issel captured the league's scoring title with an average of nearly 30 points a game, beating out former NBA standout Rick Barry of the New York Nets. Issel and Charlie Scott of Virginia shared ABA's Rookie of the Year honors.

Ramsey liked Issel's work ethics. "He was one of those people that they said was not big enough to play center at 6-9," he said. "Dan had a tremendous attitude about practice and working. They said he was too slow and couldn't jump, but by golly look what he's done. He is now in the basketball Hall of Fame. He had a tremendous career at Denver after the ABA (merged with the NBA). Dan is one fine individual."

By the way, the Squires were coached by Al Bianchi, a former boss of current UK coach Rick Pitino when they worked in New York in the NBA. Bianchi served as the New York general manager during Pitino's two years with the Knicks in late 1980s.

During Ramsey's stint with the Colonels, he coached or worked with several people from UK. They include a pair of Fabulous Five members — Ralph Beard (team scout) and Groza, guard Louie Dampier, swingman Issel, and guard Mike Pratt. Even Cawood Ledford (along with Van Vance) announced the Colonels' games on Louisville's WHAS Radio.

Overall, the 1970-71 campaign was a good one for the ABA. The league saw its attendance increased nearly 30 percent from the previous season. The Colonels had the second largest average home attendance in the ABA with 7,500 fans. Kentucky's rival, Indiana, posted the best attendance record, averaging over 8,100.

ABA's future became brighter. The young league started to get the top college players, including 7-2 Artis Gilmore, who signed with the Colonels.

But Ramsey didn't stay in the coaching business very long as he quit his post after the season. He would not be around to watch the Colonels and the league grow the following season.

"At the end of the year I had to decide whether to stay in coaching or in business," he explained. "It was very difficult. I was having to drive and fly, drive and fly.

I couldn't coach with my business interests (in Madisonville). My family was still in Madisonville. I only had a hotel room in Louisville. It got to be too much. So with my children and the ages they were, and my businesses, I decided to stay in Madisonville. I've never regretted it."

He was replaced by ex-Los Angeles Laker coach Joe Mullaney, who guided the Colonels to a sparkling 68-16 mark in the 1971-72 regular season.

While at Louisville, Ramsey became embroiled in a controversy when the departing trainer Bill Antonini made a "front-page" comment to now-defunct *Louisville Times*, charging that the Colonels were having racial problems and that Ramsey was doing a poor job of coaching. And the Louisville media — the newspaper, radio and TV people — continuously talked about the racial issue all week.

The Colonels management and several black players, however, defended Ramsey. They denied Antonini's charges, saying they were not true. According to the Colonels' 1970-71 media guide, the team had seven blacks and five whites at the beginning of the season. Ramsey said that was probably the most interesting moment he had in the ABA.

"We had a trainer who made a charge that I was a racist," Ramsey recalled. "That wasn't very pleasant. When that happened, I think it solidified the team. It allowed us to go on and go to the (ABA) finals."

On his one-year coaching experience with the Colonels, Ramsey said, "It was interesting. I enjoyed coaching and working with the players. I had a wonderful group of players — Issel, Pratt, (Cincy) Powell, Walt Simon, Darel Carrier and Louie Dampier. I enjoyed being associated with them. It was a very enjoyable experience.

I'm glad I had it. My life then was not totally basketball like when I was in Boston. My life in Boston was totally basketball."

  In 1981, Ramsey received the highest honor a player or coach can have when he was named to the Basketball Hall of Fame in Springfield, Mass. At that time, he became the third representative from UK to receive the Hall of Fame honor, joining Rupp, who was inducted in 1969, and Hagan, inducted in 1977.

  But when he first received a notification that he was chosen for the honor, he didn't believe it. A Hall of Famer? No way, he thought.

  "The first thing, I thought it was a joke because the words were misspelled," Ramsey said. "I got the letter in my mailbox. I read it but I didn't think that it would ever be possible that I would be elected to the Hall of Fame. My wife was on a tour, I believe in Italy, and I thought it was a joke so I didn't say anything to anybody. Finally, I told her and then it was announced in the paper. It was extremely difficult to believe that a substitute, particularly a boy from a community of 5,000, could be elected to the Hall of Fame.

  "It was thrilling. Unbelievable. I didn't deserve it. I'm just honored to be included in such a group. (Clarence) 'Big House' Gaines who coaches in North Carolina, Hal Greer and Willis Reed were elected that year." Greer and Reed were the former NBA stars.

  Since Ramsey's induction in 1981, two more individuals with UK ties have been selected to the Hall of Fame. Joining the prestigious ranks were Dan Issel (1993) and Cawood Ledford (1994).

When the 1989-90 campaign began, UK's newly-hired coach, Rick Pitino, only had eight scholarship players. His tallest player was 6-7 junior Reggie Hanson. The probation-ridden Cats had to rebuild from the ugly scandal which saw them breaking several NCAA rules. Things were looking very bleak. Ramsey surely thought the Wildcats wouldn't amount to anything.

But Pitino stunned Ramsey and everybody else as the scrapping Cats, who led the country in three-point shooting, pulled out a near-miraculous season, finishing with a 14-14 worksheet.

"I didn't think they would win five or six games the first year," Ramsey said. "I was surprised that first year. On that group with (Richie) Farmer, (John) Pelphrey and (Deron) Feldhaus, he (Pitino) got more out of them than I thought possible. Rick plays an exciting style of basketball. He is a tremendous coach. He fits well with Kentuckians."

Besides running the bank, Ramsey also enjoys working on his farm in Dixon. Just like his former college coach, Adolph Rupp, who spent a lot of time at his family farm in central Kentucky just to get away from the daily stressful living.

"The only businesses that I am involved in are farming and banking," Ramsey said. "So I do spend a lot of time there (at the farm). Jean and I have a house on it that we spend a lot of time in. We have horses. We've got four wheelers. There's deer on it. We have a big pond full of fish that the kids fish in. It is a farmer's farm and we plant about 750 acres of soybeans and corn."

While at UK, he met Jean in their freshmen year. "We dated and married four years later," Ramsey said, proudly showing his family picture. "(We're) still married and we have three children and six grandchildren. I only have one grandson and he is 10 years old. He enjoys basketball. A year ago, when we went up to the Hall of Fame dinner (in Springfield, Mass.), I took him with me. He certainly enjoyed going."

By the way, Ramsey's mother, Sara, is a die-hard Wildcat faithful. She's in her early 90s and lives in a nursing home. "I go to see her every day," Ramsey said. "She's a big UK fan. She sits, listens and watches the games. And the next day, I get a complete (strategic) discussion of it — why Kentucky won or why Kentucky lost."

2 Rupp Runt

LARRY CONLEY

During his sophomore season at UK, 6-3 forward Larry Conley observed a 1964 incident in Nashville where his legendary coach, Adolph Rupp, made quite an impression on him. It took place in the team's locker room after the Wildcats had lost to Vanderbilt by two points, an 85-83 heartbreaker. UK had suffered its second straight setback. The coach wasn't a happy man. In fact, he was a very angry man.

"When we came in (to the dressing room) after the game was over, we were all down," recalled Conley, who is now a television commentator. "I mean we were the No. 1 team in the country and we were starting out in the conference 0 and 2. Of course, the polls changed the next week after we lost those two games. (The other loss was to then-SEC member Georgia Tech.)

"And coach Rupp just unleashed a verbal assault on all of us. There's no way you could print it. The words were just flying out of his mouth. All of a sudden, Harry Lancaster, the assistant coach, turned around and saw a writer standing over in the corner, writing all of this down. I don't know how he had gotten in there."

After noticing the writer was taking notes, Lancaster informed Rupp. Needless to say, that made Rupp madder than ever. The coach walked over to the guy and he said, "If you print one word of that, I'll have your job."

And Conley became impressed. "I thought (to myself) right then, 'This is a powerful man. This is a really powerful man,' " he said.

Political columnist George Will once called Rupp "a great coach and a bad man," and unfairly portrayed him as a coach who did not want blacks on his team.

Conley doesn't agree with the nationally-known columnist's observations as well as other writers' similar views about the legendary coach. He had a chance to observe Rupp very closely during his four years at UK and afterwards. Other than his teammates and assistant coaches, he knew Rupp more than most people. Friends, acquaintances, fans and the news media frequently ask Conley about the "Man in the Brown Suit."

Noted writer Curry Kirkpatrick of *Sports Illustrated* was one of them. The reporter wanted to know about Rupp. Especially his racial attitudes. He was preparing a feature surrounding the famous 1966 Texas Western-Kentucky game. That contest basically marked the beginning of full racial integration in college basketball. And SEC had the first black player in the league in 1966 when Vanderbilt signed future All-SEC performer Perry Wallace, who was also recruited by Kentucky.

"Did you ever hear him say the 'word,' you know?" Kirkpatrick repeatedly asked Conley.

"Curry, I never, ever heard him say that. I'm not going to say he didn't say it, but I never heard him. Now, that's the truth. Whether you want to accept the truth or not, that's your problem. But I'm telling you, I never heard him (say that)."

Conley says the national media's unfavorable portrayal of Rupp disturbs him, but not to the point where he'd have a confrontation with a sportswriter. "I think that sometimes he's unfairly portrayed for a lot of reasons," he said. "If a writer asked me, I would tell him what I knew. I mean I didn't spend every waking moment with coach Rupp. I know there are probably some things in his background that would lend itself to that because of his age and the time he grew up in.

"We sometimes have a tendency, particularly on a national level, not to really do in-depth studies on individuals where we seem to pick out the things we want to write about. To glorify, or in this situation, to crucify a man unfairly without giving both sides of it.

"I've been in the media now for almost 18 years and it's always been my policy that nobody is ever as bad as you think they are. They are somewhere in between and the thing that bothers me the most about what they write about him is the fact that they don't balance it up. They give an awful bad side, but there was a good side, too. I think every human being has their flaws. We all do. He certainly had his. But while there was a bad side, there was also a good side.

"He had a big heart for kids. No one knows the work he did with the Shriners' Hospital for children here (in Lexington). No one ever mentions that. He did work like that all the time and contributed a lot of money to that hospital."

As a player, Conley remembers Rupp as a tough disciplinarian more than anything else. Although the players proudly wore their Wildcat uniforms, they were afraid of him. Rupp intimidated them.

"He was not what I would call a positive motivator," Conley said. "He motivated more out of fear than he did out of trying to get you to accomplish something from a positive side. I'm not saying that was all bad. There were people who respond to that. When given a challenge, they would respond to the challenge. Then there were others who didn't respond well to the confrontation. Some people rebelled at that. Back in that period, coach Rupp used to run off one or two players every year. They could not stand that type of pressure or that type of coaching. Coach Rupp was a different type of individual.

"I think the influence he had on me was more out of perfection of doing a job well. It was the constant repetition of the basketball drills to the point where you were almost perfect. You were expected to be almost perfect. He was a perfectionist in his own right. He was as hard on himself as he was on his players. His players, for the most part, responded. There were some that didn't — some good ones that didn't. But, from a motivational standpoint, I'm not sure that I ever took anything away except that I wanted to go out and play because I respected him."

At UK, during his senior season of 1965-66, Conley and his scrappy teammates — none of the starters were over 6-foot-5 — became popularly known as Rupp's Runts. They had captured the imagination of the entire nation by overcoming the odds and advancing to the NCAA championship game before dropping to Texas Western (now Texas-El Paso) 72-65.

When the season began, UK was nowhere to be found in the preseason rankings. "We weren't even in the top 40, not even close," Conley said. "Things kind of broke right for us that year. We came together pretty well. Coach Rupp had had a bad year the year before. We were 15-10 and he was just not going to go out like that again. He'd had too many great years and he really drove us hard, really hard. We ended up with two-a-day practices twice a week. He never had done that before.

"We started a running program that year through (the leadership of new assistant coach) Joe Hall and by the time we had gotten to the beginning of the season, we were in great shape. We were in fantastic shape. We became a very fast team, very quick. And we just ran people down. I think, from a physical standpoint, we were just so much better and in better condition than most people."

UK's stunning loss to No. 3 Texas Western certainly surprised many fans. Kentucky had been favored to win the national championship.

"I think what happened was the people thought that when we beat Duke, which was No. 2, that was it," explained Conley. "It was going to be over. But Texas Western was ranked third and we were first. We knew they were going to be good. They wouldn't have been there (in the title game) if they hadn't been good."

The setback practically devastated the team, which finished with a sparkling 27-2 mark. Some say it was Rupp's most disappointing loss of his coaching career.

"It was the only thing in my life that I'd change," Conley commented. "I would love to have won that game. Everybody makes a racial thing out of that game, but it was not racial for us. I mean, very frankly, if I could have kicked their ass, I would have kicked their ass — white or black. It made no difference to me. It was the championship game. It was important to us. It's important to the black people of America. If they have to hang their hat on that as something to look back to, that's okay.

"I would tell you this, though, if I could play it every year, I'd play it every year and go back just to win it. It was an important game to me. It was my last year. But I don't dwell on it. Life goes on."

In that contest, Conley and Pat Riley were not up to par. Conley was ill and Riley had problems with his foot. Conley said he was "pretty sick. I had the flu. I had gotten it the weekend before at the University of Iowa (in the NCAA Mideast Regional). It was very cold. We were home on Sunday and I started feeling really bad. I didn't practice all week. I was out from Sunday and on. In practice all I did was just dress and go out there and sit around. I didn't do much of anything.

"I had like three or four shots of penicillin. Dr. (V.A.) Jackson gave the worst shots of anybody I had ever seen. I joke with him about that (he laughed). But I was sick. It was one of those nights where things just did not go well for us."

Conley — who also played baseball at UK — finished the campaign with an 11.5-point average, fourth highest on the squad, and earned All-SEC honors. The 6-3 Riley led the Wildcats in scoring with an average of nearly 22 points.

Besides Conley and Riley, the other starters on that 1965-66 squad were 6-5 guard Tommy Kron (who was Conley's roommate and closest friend on the team), 6-0 guard Louie Dampier and 6-5 center Thad Jaracz. All five made various All-SEC teams. Riley and Dampier were also named All-Americans.

The famed "Rupp's Runts" team had seven players from the state of Kentucky. Being from Ashland, Conley was one of them. Since he was a true Kentuckian, the Wildcat program had always been very special for Conley. After all, he grew up hearing about Rupp and UK. He was fascinated with UK basketball.

"I grew up in Kentucky and I had known Kentucky since I was old enough to dribble a basketball," Conley said. "There was something intrinsic in that to me. That transcended even coach Rupp. It was Kentucky basketball. I was an 18-year-old kid who wanted to carry on that tradition. (Kentucky) is a very poor state, comparatively speaking of other states around the country, and one of the things they (Kentuckians) have always clung to has been the Kentucky basketball program. It's a source of pride and if you grew up with that, you don't ever get away from it. And that's what it was for me. It was a loyalty thing. I wanted to play. I wanted to do well for a lot of reasons — for myself, my family and for the people in the state. It's just a feeling that you have. And I was a part of an important program."

Riley, who resigned as the New York Knicks head coach in June of 1995, is still one of the NBA's all-time winningest coaches today. In the 1980s, Riley captured four NBA titles when he coached the Los Angeles Lakers.

But Conley never dreamed that his former UK teammate would be a big-time coach. "I never thought he would be an NBA coach," he said. "It's funny how all of this has transpired over the years. As a pro player, he was a journeyman. I mean he basically played with four or five different clubs during his NBA (playing) career. Then after he finished, he actually went to the radio and was working with (announcer) Chick Hearn, doing the Lakers' games. When Paul Westhead got the ax, they were looking for a coach. And Pat just kind of stepped into it. It was almost by accident that he got the job. I don't think there's anybody in the NBA who's done a better job coaching than Pat. I think he's done a terrific job."

During the 1993-94 campaign, when New York went all the way to the NBA Finals before losing to Houston, Riley did perhaps the best coaching job of his career, according to Conley.

Conley was impressed because "I thought the team he had was very mediocre. They had a great center (Patrick Ewing) and a bunch of guys who just kind of filled in. He got them to play hard, which is the key in the NBA. If you're going to coach those guys, you've got to get them to play hard because they don't have any motivation. They've got all the money they need. They just play for pride and Pat's very good at that. He can motivate people."

Not only did Conley excel on the hardwood floor, he was also good in the classroom. He was a serious student with a "B" average and made the Academic All-SEC teams in 1964 and '65. He had plans for a career in dentistry, but it didn't pan out that way.

"I started out as a major in pre-dental," Conley said. "I switched to a political science major after about my second year. I ended up graduating with a major in political science and a minor in economics and chemistry. So I really had everything. I just crossed the board."

Conley even went to law school at UK for one year. However, he has no regrets about dropping out of the graduate school. "I just didn't feel comfortable," he said. "A lot of those guys whom I went to law school with are now running the state. They're judges and lawyers in their communities and are doing very well. And I made some wonderful friends while I was there."

After leaving UK, he decided to play pro basketball. Conley wasn't drafted by anyone, but he wanted to try his luck in the pro ranks. He made the season-opening roster with the Kentucky Colonels of the new American Basketball Association. In addition to Conley, the Colonels had a couple of other former UK teammates in Louie Dampier and Cotton Nash.

But Conley didn't stay in pro basketball very long. A member of the National Guard, he had to join the Army during a riotous period when the United States fought in the Vietnam Conflict in the late 1960s. It was an experience he will never forget.

"I got one game into the season and I got my

notice," Conley said. "I was shipped to Fort Polk, Louisiana and did my basic training there and I did my infantry training at Fort Dix, New Jersey. By the time I had finished all that training, that year was over with. The basketball year was over.

"It was also at a time when (Richard) Nixon was elected (President) in 1968. This was in the 1968 and '69 era, and when I look back on history, those two years have a lot of meaning to me. Those two years stand out more to me than any two years I think I'll ever remember in my lifetime only because of all the turmoil that went on. And he (Nixon) had made the promise about withdrawing the troops from Vietnam. After I had been in (the service) for about a year, they started pulling out of there. So things kind of worked in reverse for me. I didn't go over. I ended up staying here in this country and finished out my training in the Army.

"It was such a turbulent period. We questioned everything that happened. We questioned authority. I can remember everything that went on at (UK) campus here, and our campus was fairly mild compared to some of the other ones around the country. It was certainly an interesting period."

That one game with the Colonels, by the way, was the only one Conley played in his very brief pro career. And, interestingly, that was the Colonels' first contest ever in the history of the franchise. Conley played 18 minutes, scoring only two points, in a 117-95 loss to the host Indiana Pacers before a sellout crowd of over 9,000 at the State Fairgrounds Coliseum. Cotton Nash poured in 14 points and had 10 rebounds for the Colonels, who were paced by a 24-point, 13-rebound performance by ex-Murray State standout Stewart Johnson.

"I remember we had a big house that night," Conley commented. "It was crowded. And (former NBA star) George Mikan was the first commissioner of the ABA. He came to the game and said, 'This is really a historic moment.' He came into our locker room and talked to us. It was really interesting."

On using ABA's innovative red-white-blue basketball, Conley said he never got used to it. "(The ball) was
the strangest thing to shoot with and you watch it twirl,"
he said. "It was like a kaleidoscope. You sit here and
watch it and it'd just spin and spin."

Conley, meanwhile, has become a member of
"Who's Who" club. He is one of a handful of individuals
who have played only one pro basketball game.

"Somebody said I was one of the nine players ever
to play one professional basketball game," said Conley.
"I'll tell you another guy (on the list) by the name of Jack
McCloskey, the ex-general manager for (NBA's Minnesota)
Timberwolves. I didn't know many of the other guys. It
was in an article a guy sent to me the other day.
Somebody out of Kansas City had written the article."

After his stint in the Army, Conley spent only one
year (1968-69) in coaching basketball at George
Washington University in Washington, D.C. He served as
an assistant to head coach Wayne Dobbs, who later took a
similar post at Vanderbilt. Conley was also an assistant
in baseball. Conley wasn't the only Kentucky connection
on the GWU roundball squad, which also had senior Bob
Tallent, a transfer from UK, on its playing roster. (During
his only season at GWU, Tallent averaged nearly 30 points
a game. He later became the head coach at GWU for
seven years.)

The city of Washington, D.C., will always hold a
warm spot in Conley's heart. "I had a great time in
Washington," he recalled. "I was single. I met my wife (on
a recruiting trip in New York). It was a great city to be in
during that period. There's something about Washington
that rejuvenates me, gets my blood going. It's just a
remarkable place. Everytime I go back, I see some of the
same things over and over again. When I lived there, I

was the biggest tourist. I went to all the monuments.

"(Recently) I had (broadcasted) a game with Maryland and Georgetown, and I actually stayed over two extra days so I could go by and see some of the museums I hadn't seen before. I think Washington is one of our really great cities. It's a shame that it gets the rap because I think it's a beautiful place."

After he got out of coaching, Conley moved on to Converse Rubber Company where he was a sales representative. "I just decided there were better things for me out there," he said. Later, he worked at General Electric Credit Corporation in Atlanta as a regional vice-president in addition to his broadcasting duties.

Conley currently makes his home in Atlanta with his family. His wife, Lorie, whom he met in New York, is originally from Minnesota. They have two sons, Chris and Ryan. Chris is a recent graduate of Florida Southern College in Lakeland where he played varsity basketball. Ryan was attending the College of Charleston in South Carolina.

In the early 1970s, when Conley first began broadcasting games on TV, he didn't receive any paychecks. But the experience he gained certainly helped him get a job as an announcer on regional telecasts.

"I first started doing college basketball games for the PBS station in the state of Georgia," Conley recalled. "I did University of Georgia basketball games for no fee. Nobody paid me anything. I just went over and did them, and had a lot of fun doing it."

Conley credits a couple of individuals for giving him a chance to work the SEC games on regional television. Helping Conley were former TV commentator Joe Dean Sr. (now the LSU athletic director) and current Chicago White Sox owner Eddie Einhorn. Conley's first

SEC telecast was the Florida-Vanderbilt game at Gainesville in 1977.

Conley said, "At the time, Joe was the Southeastern Conference basketball announcer on TVS (network) and TVS had sold the rights of their basketball package to NBC. And Joe had worked with a guy by the name of Eddie Einhorn, who started TVS. In fact, he (Einhorn) started the SEC as his first package. They had a doubleheader one day and Joe told Eddie, 'Why don't you give Larry a try?' So he (Einhorn) called me up and asked me to do a game."

Several days after broadcasting his first regional TV game, Conley received a complimentary letter. It was from Einhorn. "You did a nice job," Einhorn wrote. "I think we'll have you back if we get another market (outside SEC)."

And Conley got paid for that game. "Two hundred dollars," he smiled. The former Wildcat said his broadcasting fee today is "a little bit better."

Back then, there was one other television market that TVS did not cover in college basketball — the Atlantic Coast Conference area. In the following season, Einhorn decided to raid the ACC television market, competing against the likes of North Carolina, Virginia, North Carolina State, Duke, among others, by doing a series of TV games in the Southern Conference and two independents — South Carolina and Virginia Tech. Conley became one of the regular announcers.

"It was back in the cave stone or cave era when all they had was one game a week," Conley said. "It was on Saturdays. Of course, that's changed a lot now. But that's how I got started."

Conley sometimes covers his alma mater on regional or national television. Some Kentucky fans, ironically, have accused him of showing favoritism toward UK's opponent. He said most of the critical or negative letters come from the Wildcat fans. "It's unbelievable," Conley quipped.

For a couple of years in late 1980s, Conley and

Marty Brennaman (the Voice of the Cincinnati Reds) broadcasted several Kentucky games on the UK Television Basketball Network. Conley said he and Brennaman had an excellent working relationship and enjoyed covering UK games. They were disappointed when UK let them go after the 1988-89 season. Brennaman later claimed politics played a key role in his dismissal from the UK network.

February 15, 1994.
The Miracle of Mardi Gras.
That was the night Kentucky rallied from a 31-point deficit in the second half to defeat LSU 99-95 in the biggest comeback in school history. And the exciting matchup game was called by none other than Conley on a late-night ESPN telecast.

"The LSU-Kentucky game in Baton Rouge was the most memorable game I've ever been involved with," Conley said of his sportscasting career. "I sat there in disbelief that a team could be down 31 points with 15 and one-half minutes to go and still win a game. I mean it was like being in a dream. You're sitting there, you're watching it happen, but you don't believe that it's happening."

Since the game, headed for a blowout, was late in the evening, many fans went to bed, thinking UK had lost the game. "For those people who got up the next morning and saw the score, they were probably as much in disbelief as I was," Conley smiled. "I've had a lot of great games over the years. But certainly that game would go down in my book as probably the most memorable."

Neither Conley nor his broadcasting partner, Brad Nessler, interviewed Rick Pitino, the winning coach, and his players on TV after the game because it ran too late. "It was an ESPN game and we were already running long so we had to go to the SportsCenter," explained the announcer. "We were way over our time limit."

However, Conley's comments on the wild Kentucky-LSU game were made before the 1995 SEC Tournament in Atlanta. Another TV thriller had taken place. He and partner Tom Hammond, who is also a UK graduate, covered the SEC Tournament championship showdown between national powers Kentucky and Arkansas. As every Wildcat fan knows, UK had bounced back from a 19-point, first-half deficit as well as nine-point overtime deficit to defeat the Hogs 95-93 in a dramatic fashion. That 1995 matchup certainly ranks as one of the most exciting UK games ever. Afterwards, a jubilant Pitino told reporters this was the proudest moment of his coaching career.

Conley grew up in Ashland in northeastern Kentucky. He comes from a very sports-minded family. His father, George Conley, was the basketball coach at Ashland High School for several years in the early 1950s and later became a college basketball official in several leagues, including the Southeastern Conference. His brother and two of his sisters also played organized sports.

When the elder Conley officiated in the late 1950s, he took his teenage son on several road trips. "He took me to a couple of Tennessee games and a couple of Vanderbilt games," said the younger Conley.

But one game he fondly remembers took place in Lexington. It was during the 1957-58 campaign. The Year of the Fiddlin' Five.

"When I was a youngster, one of the most memorable games I ever saw Kentucky play was the year it won the national championship in 1958," he said. "My dad refereed a game between Temple and Kentucky (on Dec. 7) here in Lexington. It was a triple-overtime game. Vernon Hatton and his (mid-court) shot sent it to the second overtime. Temple had a great team that year. Kentucky beat them (85-83) in three overtimes. I can still see that game and that's what, 36 years ago? Later UK ended up in the semifinals of the national championship, beating Temple again."

At that time, the elder Conley was allowed to officiate UK's non-league matchups even though he was from Ashland, Conley said. "They had allowed him to referee games which were not conference games," he said.

Because of his father's travels, Conley did not see his dad very often in the winter time. "When I was growing up, I didn't see very much of my dad during the basketball season because he was refereeing," he said. "He was never home. I mean he stayed gone. He'd referee three, four or five games a week and we'd see him maybe one day a week, maybe even once every two weeks.

"Of course, I was busy. I was playing basketball by that time and he didn't get a chance to see me play very much. He just got to see a couple of the games."

When Conley went to Kentucky in 1962, his dad had to quit officiating in the SEC. But he continued to call the games as he went to the Atlantic Coast Conference. But "after I left Kentucky, he had a balanced schedule between the SEC and the ACC," said Conley.

While his dad blew whistles, he became involved in state politics. "He was in the State Senate from 1960 to '64," said the younger Conley. "He ran for state treasurer in '64 and got beat. And he was out of politics after that."

Before coming to UK, Conley starred at basketball tradition-rich Ashland High where he was an All-Stater. During his junior year, Conley and his highly-regarded Ashland squad, coached by Bob Wright, won the Sweet Sixteen title in 1961, and almost won it again the following season, losing to St. Xavier of Louisville by four points in the championship game. Interestingly, Conley was a graduating member of the last high school class (1962) at Ashland as it became Paul Blazer High School the following season.

An opinionated Conley has strong feelings on some topics involving basketball.

On numerous NCAA rules: "Competitiveness of recruiting and trying to put together winning athletic programs today are tremendous. The pressures, because of the money, have grown exponentially to the point where it has become very, very difficult not to have the rules. There's a basketball coach out there who's making a half a million dollars. He needs to perpetuate his program to continue to make that money. So the downward pressure to continue recruiting quality athletes, to bend the rules, to cheat — the temptation — is unbelievable. I'm very concerned about that.

"I know the NCAA has instituted new rules in spreading the monies that it now takes around the various schools. They can kind of try to alleviate that, but that's not going to go away. Those salaries, perks, and extra contracts from the shoe companies and the camps are going to continue to escalate. The pressures will continue to mount.

"If you don't have the rules, I think it would be like the wild west. It would just be open season. So I think you need the rules, but you need some sort of balance in the way you approach those rules. NCAA, right now, has instituted some very bad decisions on recruiting rules. Why should they try to restrict coaches from watching the players? Why would they make them stay home? All that's doing is diminishing the quality of their work. And if the quality of their work improves, that's going to give more kids opportunities for scholarships. There are lots of youngsters out there who never get a look because the NCAA has instituted rules that don't allow the coaches to get out and see a lot of players. I struggle with that a little bit.

"I think they ought to have the committee — which

reviews these rules every year — study the rules over and see if they make sense. And the academicians should not be doing it (on the committee). I think the athletics (department personnel) ought to be the ones who sit down and do it because they can police themselves. You know, given the opportunity, most of them are above board and want to play by the rules. Not all of them, but I think most of them will."

On freshman eligibility: "I'm one of those guys who think they ought to have that one year of freshman basketball. We'll never see that again, though, because of the budgetary situation involved in the college athletics. It would mean more scholarships. Presently, you have to fund the teams at the 13-scholarship level on a varsity team. (But if the freshman ineligibility concept returns), they would have another three, four or five for the freshman team. I happen to think that it's a good idea to have that one year of transition. I think it's very important.

"The problem you've got today is that the really good stars — the bona fide top 30 or 40 players in the country — will only be around for a year or two (before going to the NBA). At the most, three years. Never more than that. So you don't really get an opportunity to develop an understanding or a feeling for these players because they don't stay as long as they used to. We used to stay four years and everybody got to know everybody.

"Take Glenn Robinson as an example. He's a Prop 48 who had to sit out his first year. He comes in and plays a great second year. After his third year, he's gone. The Purdue people had him for two years. So yeah, I like the freshman teams." (Robinson, who was the NBA's top draft pick in 1994, signed a 10-year, $68 million contract with the Milwaukee Bucks.)

On UK's basketball program: "I don't know if it has changed that much. When I think about the program, I think about 'The Program.' The emphasis is still there. The adulation is still there. It's just gotten more magnified. The scrutiny of the program has continued to be at a level that no one else can ever imagine around the country. I'd say the only other place like Kentucky is North Carolina, but nowhere else. Kentucky basketball is really special. Arkansas could be. They may be on the verge of getting it like that. But they've got a couple of decades to go before they do it."

On UK players being overexposed by the media: "It seems to go with the program. It's something that's been going on since coach Rupp got up and made us successful. You could ask the same question of the people in Florida State football. Are they overexposed? I don't know. I think the media does what they have to do with something that people are interested in seeing (or reading about). Three and a half million people follow Kentucky basketball. They want to know about the team. And they're going to get fed through the media all they want to know about Kentucky basketball. It seems to perpetuate itself."

On the 64-team NCAA tournament: "It's got enough teams. I sometimes think we may have too many of them. It's somewhat watered down. Very seldom you will see the No. 14-, 15- or 16-seeded team be able to knock off a No. 1, 2 or 3 team. It happens once in a while, but not very often."

On pro basketball versus college basketball: "The games are different. There are some significant rules differences. The style of the game is much different at the NBA level than it is at the college level. I'm somewhat of a purist and there are things in the NBA game that have more of an entertainment value. They allow players to do things that I don't think they'd get away with in college. For example, it seems like every time I watch a pro basketball on TV, I see guys walk. They'll take three or four steps and nobody blows the whistle.

"Their motivation is to entertain and they don't want any stoppage in play. If they have stoppage in play, that stops the entertainment. I understand their motivation. But I think pro basketball is great fun, particularly when you get down to the end of the season and to the playoffs."

3 Golden Boy
COTTON NASH

In 1962, when *Sports Illustrated* magazine hit the newsstands with its special preseason college basketball issue, Wildcat junior Cotton Nash found himself on the magazine's cover. Nash, who had been named All-American the season before as a 6-5 sophomore, was certainly pleased with the coverage.

"I had been reading that magazine since I was a kid and here I was on the cover so I felt good," he recalled. "It was very flattering."

Even though the magazine had previously sent a photographer to the UK campus for its special roundball edition, making the cover was somewhat of a pleasant surprise for the Kentucky star. "They had come for a picture shoot several weeks prior to that so I knew it was for the basketball issue," Nash said. "I didn't know I would make the cover. I was dearly impressed."

Almost 35 years later, Nash still gets autograph requests for that cover picture. "A fan just sent me a copy of the front cover that they had saved and wanted me to autograph it and return it to them. So I still get those in the mail."

What did coach Adolph Rupp — who later made the cover of *Sports Illustrated* in 1966 during the memorable campaign of Rupp's Runts — have to say about Nash's cover photo? Not much, according to Nash. "I don't remember there being much said about anything," said the player. "Kentucky basketball was back on top and they (coaches) were all used to that (national media coverage) so I don't guess they treated that (cover) as a big deal."

While Nash was a highly-sought basketball star from Lake Charles High School in Louisiana, Rupp flew down to visit the player and his parents at their home on a recruiting trip. Rupp wanted Nash to play at UK.

"Coach Rupp ate supper with us, talked with us for the evening and was very personable," recalled the cigar-smoking Nash in a 1994 interview at his Lexington home. "He told me a lot about the attitude and the atmosphere in Lexington. I had never been to Lexington before. I did later make a campus visit and learned a lot more about Lexington.

"My first impression of coach Rupp was that he was a nice ordinary guy which, of course, later changed. At that time I was basing my decision more on the school and not his personality. I was happy that I got to play for the man who was and probably still is considered the best collegiate coach ever, along with John Wooden. I was really fortunate to play for the best."

But Rupp was not the only coach who wanted the blond-haired kid. He had competition. UCLA mentor John Wooden — who later began a string of 10 NCAA championships in 12 years, starting in 1964 — sought Nash, too. UCLA was especially aggressive in its recruiting efforts.

"John Wooden himself didn't visit, but he sent his assistants," Nash said. "He had me flown out twice, at least that I can remember, to visit the UCLA campus. At that time, there were unlimited campus visits allowed. They were on the phone every evening talking with me and trying to get me to come back out to visit again. They were my heaviest and hottest pursuer. It was really quite ironic that my senior year at UK was the first year that Wooden won his first NCAA title. So he didn't really need me after all." In addition to Kentucky and UCLA, Nash seriously considered Saint Louis and Michigan State, among others.

One of UK's 1947-48 "Fabulous Five" standouts played a key role in the recruitment of Nash for the Wildcats. Cliff Barker, an Indiana native who helped UK win two NCAA championships, was one of Nash's coaches in high school. "I really enjoyed playing for him at the time and he was a subtle influence, probably more than I realized when I did make my final decision," commented Nash.

Although Nash played at three different high schools in three states, Barker coached the player as a rising sophomore star at Jeff High in Jeffersonville, Indiana and continued to stay in touch after Nash moved to Texas and then Louisiana. "He (Barker) helped recruit me," Nash said. "In fact, at Adolph's urging, he was involved in the recruiting process. He said that I had the ability to play college ball, that coach Rupp was the best coach and that's where I should be."

Basketball wasn't the only sport Nash played in high school. He excelled in several sports. And many schools recruited him for both basketball and football. But the roundball sport eventually won out. Nash knew which college he wanted to go to if he played basketball in the Southeastern Conference. In the SEC, "there was only one place to come and that was Kentucky," he said. "That would be the biggest challenge and the biggest opportunity to prove what you could do."

Nash also had the talent to play baseball. "I had the opportunity to sign with professional baseball after I graduated from high school," he said. "There was no draft at the time, so anybody could offer you a contract. There were three or four teams which offered me an opportunity to play but it wasn't as enticing as going to college. There was no big (signing) bonus at the time. It was just the opportunity to play with a modest bonus at the time. It was nothing comparable to a college scholarship, so the decision was easy at that point."

Nash never did pay much attention to basketball when he was in his early teens. He discovered the sport when his family moved to basketball-crazed Indiana from New Jersey. "I never knew what a basketball was until I moved to Indiana," Nash commented. "I was a teenager by then and in New Jersey there was only one sport that you played and that was baseball. We didn't know that there was such a game as that big ball you bounce with.

"When I finally played basketball in Indiana, I fell in love with the sport. The enthusiasm in Indiana was such that my high school had a 5,000-seat gym. Every game sold out and they even scalped the tickets outside for the games."

When his dad, Frank Nash, had to change jobs, the family moved to Texas. But there was a problem. The younger Nash could not play high school basketball or football due to a state transfer rule. "Out-of-state transfers were made to sit out a year in football and basketball and we didn't know it at the time," Nash said. So, after spending one semester at Orange High in Texas, playing baseball, the Nash family found a solution. They moved to nearby Lake Charles in Louisiana.

"We went 35 miles across the border to Louisiana so I could play my junior and senior year in football and basketball," Nash said. "Louisiana didn't have that (transfer) rule. He (his father) commuted every day to work (in Orange, Texas) which was a real burden on him.

He really made a sacrifice in that respect but it did pay off. We just kept moving until we found the right place."

But the younger Nash became somewhat down-hearted after learning that the folks in Louisiana didn't care much for basketball. "I was disappointed when I moved to Louisiana," he said. "The emphasis was on football. There was hardly anybody at the basketball games down there. It was a dramatic change for me."

Nash had several big moments at Kentucky. When he finished his Wildcat career, the three-time All-American scored a total of 1,770 points in becoming the school's all-time leading scorer, just ahead of Fabulous Five member Alex Groza, who had 1,744 points.

And he will never forget one particular period — the Christmas holidays — during his senior year when UK returned to its glorious status as the nation's No. 1 squad. Kentucky had become the top-ranked club in the polls for the first time in several years after it defeated Notre Dame 101-81 at Louisville. And a few days later, the undefeated Wildcats improved their mark to 10-0 as they captured the Sugar Bowl tournament championship at Loyola Fieldhouse in New Orleans, beating Duke 81-79. Nash, who was named the tourney's Most Valuable Player, took the title game's scoring honors as he gunned in 30 points. Duke star Jeff Mullins, a Lexington native, pumped in 26 points in a losing cause.

"The feeling (of being at the top) was probably the best I ever had because I helped bring Kentucky basket-ball back to the top," Nash said. "From the time Kentucky won the national title in 1958 up to my senior year, the program was pretty much down by Kentucky standards. (But) I didn't think the program was down. It's like Notre Dame football. If you lose two games, your program's down."

But he nearly quit the squad while in New Orleans, preparing for the Sugar Bowl tourney. That's because the team didn't have tickets for his parents and sister, who had driven a long distance from Massachusetts to see their favorite player.

"My parents made a trip every holiday season because my dad couldn't get any time off to see me play," Nash said. "My dad was in Massachusetts and had driven down to Lexington to see the holiday tournament (UKIT) and stayed long enough to see the Sugar Bowl tournament. The trip had been a over thousand miles from Massachusetts. So when the team got to New Orleans, I automatically assumed that we would get tickets for our families."

But Rupp said there were no tickets left. And a frustrated Nash got mad.

"I lost my cool," Nash recalled. "I knew there were some available. Finally, I just said that if I couldn't get tickets I would just take them (his family) out for a movie and show them a good time. I don't know if I was serious. I was just kind of angry."

Rupp's long-time assistant, Harry Lancaster, finally delivered the tickets for the Nash family. "About an hour later, he came up to my room, knocked on the door and just handed me four tickets. He didn't say a word and left. We solved that problem."

Besides playing sports, another important chapter in Nash's life took place at UK where he met his future wife, Julie. And the couple would later have three children — Richey, Matt and Audrey. "My wife is from Mt. Sterling (Ky.) and we've been married for almost 30 years," he said.

Nash admits that he and Rupp didn't always see eye to eye. It wasn't great, but it wasn't bad, either.

"It was up and down," Nash said of his relationship with the Baron. "We had a good relationship for a while. My sophomore year was good as I broke many records. And I wanted to top my sophomore year (performance), which was probably impossible. I played with a bunch of injuries in my junior year. I sprained ankles. I had a deep bruise in my foot which at times I couldn't even walk on it. The only solution back then was Novocain. They gave me a shot.

"Rupp felt I wasn't producing with 100 percent effort and I wasn't because of my injuries. He couldn't understand that. We got into several fights, you might say. But we straightened it all out and had a good relationship my senior year."

As a sophomore, Nash led the SEC in scoring with a 23.8-point average. And he later won his second scoring title in the conference, averaging 24 points, as a senior during UK's 21-6 season.

But Rupp and his coaching staff weren't really satisfied with Nash. They thought the star player should've done more, believing that he goofed off too much on the court. That's not so, according to one of Nash's teammates.

"Cotton Nash was so talented and he moved on the floor with such fluid ease that the coaches thought he was loafing," said former All-SEC standout Larry Pursiful. "They thought he wasn't trying. He moved so easily that they thought he wasn't hustling. Cotton Nash did not have a big ego."

For six years, from 1964 to 1970, Nash held UK's all-time leading scoring record. He saw his career mark broken in 1970 when All-American Dan Issel hit a school-record 53 points in a 120-85 victory over host Ole Miss.

"I knew it wouldn't last forever," Nash said.

"Several years later, I talked with Dan. He told me when he was being recruited at Kentucky that Adolph (Rupp) had promised him that if he would come (to Kentucky), he would get a chance to break my record. As I watched Dan's career at Kentucky, it did become obvious that Adolph was fulfilling that promise."

Issel later wrote in his 1985 book, *Parting Shots*, that Rupp was pleased to see him break Nash's career record because the demanding coach wasn't very fond of Nash.

Currently, Issel remains as the men's leading career scorer in UK history with 2,138 points, averaging nearly 26 points in three years. Former All-American Kenny Walker is second on the UK career list with a four-year total of 2,080 points.

Besides scoring, Nash was also an outstanding rebounder, ranking fifth on UK's all-time list with 962 rebounds. He also holds the school's second-highest game total in rebounding with 30 snatches (against Temple in 1961 and Mississippi in 1964).

Basketball was not the only sport Nash played in collegiate ranks. Like his high school days, he participated in several sports. He was a true athlete.

"I played both baseball and basketball and was on the track team for a couple of years," Nash said. "Rupp did not care about us playing other sports. At the time, we had four or five other players who played both sports. That was when collegiate sports were still a sport and not a big business."

And Nash saw plenty of Harry Lancaster on the UK campus. Lancaster had two jobs, serving as the head baseball coach in addition to being an assistant on Rupp's coaching staff.

"I thought Harry was an important part of Rupp's

success (in basketball)," Nash said. "If he didn't have Harry as an assistant all those years, I'm not sure how his record would have turned out. I give a lot of credit to Harry Lancaster.

"Rupp and Harry did have a lot of similarities but they always played the good guy and bad guy routine or cops where Adolph would be the bad cop and Harry the good cop. Harry often acted as Adolph's executioner, too. The hatchet man. When somebody needed straightening out in a big way, Adolph would send Harry to do it. He was very versatile for Adolph and he was also very charming."

Later, just like the former star Bo Jackson who participated in two pro sports (football and baseball), Nash played major league baseball and pro basketball.

"*The Sporting News* had an article a few years back and I was surprised to see the number of athletes who played both sports," Nash commented. "There were only about a dozen or so players who played both baseball and basketball. There were more who played both football and baseball. I don't think you can compare me to Bo Jackson. That is two different situations."

In pro baseball, Nash began in the California Angels' farm system before he was shipped to the Chicago White Sox in a 1967 trade involving veteran first baseman Bill "Moose" Skowron of Chicago. (Earlier in his career, Skowron had played in eight World Series championships, including seven with the New York Yankees.) Nash briefly played for the White Sox that season in a reserve role. Two years later, he appeared in the major leagues again with a different organization, the Minnesota Twins, in 1969 and '70.

"I wasn't in the big leagues that long to really have any great moments," he said. A backup outfielder and first baseman, Nash played only 13 games with 16 at-bats in his career, hitting for an average of .188.

One of Nash's big-league managers was none other than controversial figure Billy Martin, who directed the Twins (97-65) to the 1969 American League West Division championship as a rookie manager. "Billy Martin was a player's manager," Nash said. "If a player had to pick a guy they wanted as their manager, the majority of them would say they wanted Billy Martin. He was not a front office manager. He couldn't get along with any front office. He always had conflict with the front office but he was the best in relating to the players. And it was an experience just to play for him."

In 1964, the Los Angeles Lakers, coming off a 42-38 season, made Nash their second-round NBA draft pick. UCLA star Walt Hazzard was the team's first round pick. And the Lakers, by the way, had future Hall of Famers Jerry West and Elgin Baylor on their roster.

"I'm not really sure that the Lakers really wanted me at the time," said Nash, whose Wildcat jersey was retired by UK in 1991. "Most teams were hesitant to draft me when they found out I was going to play two sports out of college. A lot of baseball teams were hesitant to talk to me or offer me a contract because I was going to play basketball and the same went with the NBA teams.

"I should have been the first round choice but I wasn't because of that fact. The Lakers drafted me as an insurance policy because Elgin Baylor had been complaining or had knee problems the year before. During the exhibition season, I did a lot of games. I started a lot in Elgin's place. He limped along during the exhibition season which was about 20 games long. When the regular season started, something miraculous happened. His knees were just fine. He became healthy again. My role diminished because I was there as his insurance policy. They got rid of me (during the season) and I had signed with the (California) Angels."

After playing 25 games, averaging 2.1 points, for the Lakers, he went to the struggling San Francisco (now Golden State) Warriors who would eventually finish with a woeful 17-63 mark for the 1964-65 season. Nash completed his first NBA season with a 3.0-point average in 45 games.

And he returned to baseball, trying his luck with the Angels organization. "I saw where the two-sport situation was taking away (my concentration and time) from both of them," Nash explained. "It was getting to be impossible to do justice for either sport. I had to make a choice so I chose baseball."

But two years later, a new pro basketball team came calling in 1967. The ABA's Kentucky Colonels pursued Nash. The club owner, Joseph Gregory, wanted him. He needed someone with a drawing power at the gate. Nash certainly fit the bill as he was a former All-American at UK. At first, Nash said no; he wasn't interested. But Gregory wouldn't give up.

"They kept calling me all summer," Nash recalled. "I thought it over and I gave them a figure that I would sign for and I thought that would get rid of them. I didn't hear from them for a couple of weeks. Then about September, they agreed to my terms. So I said, 'What the hell, I might as well play.' I played my last game of the season in baseball and then I played with the Colonels in Louisville. I didn't play the entire (1967-68 roundball) season as the White Sox camp was calling me to come for the spring training.

"I thought I had made an error in judgment in trying to go back to basketball again. I left the season a few weeks early to go back to baseball. The next year I had a poor season (in baseball) so I guess I proved myself right."

Asked about his salary with the Colonels, Nash smiled, "I'm not going to tell you what I made." But Nash reportedly was the highest-paid player on the squad in the

neighborhood of $20,000. His high-scoring teammate, for-
mer UK All-American Louie Dampier, said he himself
earned $15,000, including a $2,500 bonus.

His only season with the Colonels was certainly
interesting. "The league wasn't very well organized the
first year," Nash said. "I remember playing one game in a
hockey arena and they had laid the floor over the ice. The
moisture settled on the floor and you could hardly move
out there. Everybody was slipping and sliding around.
You couldn't do anything about it. You'd wipe it off now
and then, but it would come right back. We went like it
was slow motion, just tiptoeing around.

"The first strangest thing was getting used to that
ball. Playing with that red, white and blue thing looked
funny coming towards you sometimes. A lot of players had
trouble with passing and trying to catch the ball. It was
different. They had crazy promotions, but I don't remember what they were."

With the Colonels, who finished fourth in a five-
team Eastern Division with a 36-42 mark, Nash saw
action in 39 regular season games and averaged 8.5
points.

Now a businessman who owns a real estate and
investment firm in Lexington, Nash has some thoughts
about today's athletes making unbelievably-high salaries.

"I think that I was born too early," he quipped. "It's
awful. The players' salary structure shouldn't be such a
big issue (in the baseball strike of 1994 and '95). I was on
both sides of the table. I managed and coached in baseball
and from what I knew none of the owners were dumb.
They are all good businessmen. They weren't in that as a
hobby. If these guys pay it, then they can afford to pay it.
The players deserve it. The salaries aren't out of line."

Nash said he still attends some UK matchups at Rupp Arena, but he would rather stay home and watch the games on television. "I go downtown once in a while, but I let the family and the kids use the tickets mostly," he said.

He likes Kentucky mentor Rick Pitino and his running game. "I'm really pleased that they hired Pitino," Nash said. "I love his kind of ball. He's a throwback to when I played. Even though Pitino has his fast-paced offense, I'm not sure he could have kept up with some of our teams. We didn't have a three-point shot. We went to three figures (100s) at least 10 times in a 27-game schedule (in 1963-64)."

On his playing career, Nash acknowledged that most sports fans remember him for his outstanding accomplishments at Kentucky.

"I see people viewing me as a former UK player and nothing else," said the ex-Wildcat star, who has lived in Lexington permanently since 1973. "But I think it's more important to note that I was on the short list of athletes who played professional baseball and basketball. To me, that was a whole lot more to accomplish than just playing college basketball."

4 Wildcat Minister

LARRY PURSIFUL

What does ex-Kentucky star Larry Pursiful have in common with the other 1962 college basketball standouts such as Leroy Ellis (who would become the father of future UK cager LeRon Ellis), Zelmo Beaty, Jerry Lucas, Don Nelson, John Havlicek and Dave DeBusschere?

They all were drafted by the NBA teams in 1962. After Pursiful completed his senior year at third-ranked UK with first-team All-SEC honors, the Wildcat captain was one of only three SEC stars selected in the NBA draft that year.

An eighth-round draft pick by the Chicago Packers franchise (now the Washington Bullets), Pursiful was offered a one-year pact to play with the NBA club. The Chicago Packers, at that time, were an expansion franchise coming off an 18-62 mark in its inaugural season.

Shortly after the draft, the Packers mailed the guard a letter along with the contract. "We are in very dire need of good backcourt men who have the ability to lead as you can and also have the ability to shoot from the outside as our scouts have seen you do," wrote Dave Trager, a club official. "Kentucky players who have learned their basketball from Adolph Rupp have had great success in the National Basketball Association. All reports on you indicate that you are one of the outstanding guards to come out of Kentucky in the last 10 years."

But Pursiful — who was UK's second-leading scorer with 19.1 points behind teammate Cotton Nash's SEC-leading 23.4 points — wasn't interested mainly because of job security reasons.

"I had the opportunity to play with Chicago but I opted to play with a team called the Phillips 66 Oilers," he said. "I played two years with them. The NBA, at that time, was not paying anything. I've still got one of my contracts and it was $7,000 from Chicago. I didn't sign it because that would have made me a professional and the Phillips was an amateur team. They let you play and gave you a job with the Phillips Petroleum Co., the corporation. Once I finished playing, I had a job for the rest of my life if I wanted it.

"We played about 70 games every year. We had a league called the National Industrial Basketball League. It was a great league and comparable to the NBA. We played the Akron Goodyear. The Peoria Caterpillars had a team as well as the Denver Truckers. We played great teams in the Army. For advertising purposes, we played some colleges. We played UT (University of Tennessee) and Tennessee Tech. I worked about three years with Phillips after I retired from playing. I was a regional representative in Louisville."

Another team in Chicago from the new American Basketball League also wanted Pursiful. The Chicago Majors offered Pursiful a $6,000 salary.

Strangely, when Pursiful performed as an All-Stater at Bell County High School in southeastern Kentucky, only one school offered him a college basketball scholarship. And that college was Kentucky. Nobody else bothered to give the Bell County player a scholarship.

"It was kind of unusual that they (the Wildcats) were the only people who recruited me," Pursiful recalled. "That was fine with me because UK was the only place that I wanted to go. Like most Kentucky mountain boys, I grew up listening to all the great teams at Kentucky, the Fabulous Five, Ramsey and Hagan. I never really wanted to go anywhere else. When I found out that they might even slightly be interested in me, I was determined to do the best that I could do to make it."

Before coming to Bell County High for his senior year, Pursiful played three years at Lone Jack High, near his hometown of Fourmile, also in Bell County. While Pursiful was at Lone Jack, Bobby Slusher — who later played for Rupp at Kentucky — was one of his prep teammates.

Pursiful will never forget one game during his junior season when Lone Jack visited a strong Lexington Lafayette club, which had future Wildcat star Billy Ray Lickert. "We got beat by six or eight points," Pursiful commented. "But I had a good night and I remember that coach Rupp and coach (Harry) Lancaster came to watch my teammate Bobby Slusher play. After that game they started recruiting me some and I was just thrilled beyond all imagination that they might be interested in me."

Pursiful's childhood exposure to playground basketball in the early 1950s certainly helped him prepare for competition in prep and major college ranks. He loved basketball. He was crazy about the sport.

"I played basketball all of the time," he said. "I remember starting when I was in the fourth or fifth grade. I would shoot in the rain or the snow. My older brother (Darrell) was playing at that time, and he and his friends used to give me a hard time because I wanted to play with the bigger boys and they wouldn't let me. I just kept aggravating them and they wouldn't let me. But I just kept working and playing. We had an old outdoor goal down where I lived. Every time we — the boys — got together, we played. (When we weren't playing), we would go to a movie on Saturday afternoon in Pineville, but there wasn't a lot to do back then."

During his freshman year at UK, especially in the fall semester of 1958, Pursiful had a difficult time — socially, academically and athletically. He was a struggling mountain kid trying to adjust to his new life in a strange city.

"I didn't have any idea of some of the things that went on in Lexington," he recalled. "It was a big adjustment for me. The first day of practice was a major eye-opening thing with the way coach Rupp handled the players. He was very much like Bobby Knight (of Indiana) in expecting perfection. I watched and sat in on the first varsity practice my freshman year. I thought, 'Where am I?' I had never been subjected to discipline that intense.

"The year before — my senior year in high school — I had watched one game at Memorial Coliseum. Then I was in Lexington again to play in an East-West Kentucky all-star game. That was my only experience with Lexington."

For awhile, Pursiful was not the only player from Bell County in UK's basketball program. The 6-5 Slusher, his former teammate at Lone Jack, was a promising Wildcat sophomore when Pursiful arrived on the campus as a raw rookie. But Rupp later dismissed Slusher for disciplinary reasons.

"Freshmen did not play (on the varsity) and if he had stayed in school I would have gotten to play with Bobby again," Pursiful said. "Bobby was a great player and had a lot of talent. I hated to see him leave. He got into trouble, personal trouble. The last time I saw Bobby, I was playing with Phillips (in the mid 1960s) in Ironton, Ohio, and Bobby came up to the game. We talked for a long time. He was teaching (at the time)."

Like many other ex-UK players, Pursiful has many Rupp stories. Rupp often fussed at the 6-1 guard, known as a great shooter, for not shooting enough baskets.

"Coach was always on me because I wouldn't shoot," Pursiful said. "I felt like I could hit most shots when I was open. He wanted me to shoot sometimes when I felt that I wasn't open. He stayed on me about that."

One night, while Pursiful was sitting with some of the other players in the hotel lobby at Nashville (where the Cats were facing Vanderbilt), Rupp saw the mountain kid en route to the team's pre-game workout. They engaged in a brief conversation with the coach telling the youngster not to bother going in to practice.

"Fourmile, you might as well stay at the hotel tonight," moaned Rupp, who sometimes called his players by their hometown.

"What have I done now?" asked a startled Pursiful.

"You weren't going to shoot anyway so you might as well stay at the hotel," said the coach.

Pursiful certainly didn't know what to think.

Later, Rupp told Pursiful that every time the player shot the basketball, he thought it was going to go in. "Coach Rupp had a great knack for building confidence in yourself," Pursiful said. "When your coach tells you that, you can do it. Coach Rupp had some interesting stories, and was a great motivator and a great psychologist.

"Coach Lancaster did most of the game strategy and planning what we were going to do against certain teams. But coach Rupp got you motivated to play."

In December of 1959, Kentucky invaded UCLA, coached by John Wooden, and Southern California in a couple of non-conference matchups in sunny Los Angeles. While over there, Rupp had two hair-raising moments, according to Pursiful. It had nothing to do with basketball.

Recalled Pursiful, "In my sophomore year, we traveled to LA and played UCLA (in a 68-66 victory) one night and Southern California (in a 14-point loss) the next night. On Saturday night, on the way to the hotel from the Southern Cal game, a car load of people ran through a red light and the bus hit them broadside. No one was hurt.

"And the next day we went to Disneyland. There was a ride at Disneyland called the Matterhorn. It's a replica of Matterhorn mountain and it's a roller-coaster type ride. We rode and two cars behind me was coach Rupp and coach (Bernie) Shively, the athletic director. And when Rupp got off, he was white as a sheet. He shook his head, looked at Shively and said, 'I'd rather ride with that bus driver.' "

Pursiful respected Rupp so much that he obeyed every order issued by Rupp or his assistants. The loyal youngster had pride in donning the Wildcat uniform. He didn't want to cause any embarrassment to the basketball program or the school.

"The only thing that I ever did was miss curfew by maybe 15 or 20 minutes," he said. "I wanted to play so badly that I was going to follow every rule in the books and that's the truth. I wanted to play for UK so badly that I wouldn't do anything for coach Rupp or Lancaster to be on my case. I think they knew they would not have any trouble out of me breaking the rules especially after my sophomore year."

But, like most of his teammates, Pursiful was not real comfortable with Rupp. So, whenever he had a problem, he approached Lancaster.

"Coach Lancaster was easier to talk to," he said. "In all honesty, I was frightened of coach Rupp. I was in awe of him with me coming from the mountains. I knew I could talk to coach Lancaster about anything, so I would just go to him.

"I was very frightened when he (Rupp) got mad. After I graduated, I saw him a couple of times. We would talk but not have a long conversation."

Growing up in the Middlesboro area, Pursiful heard a lot of things about the Tennessee Vols, especially in football and basketball. He had to put up with a lot of "ribbing" from many Vol fans living in the tri-state area of Kentucky, Tennessee and Virginia. He didn't care for Tennessee. He loved UK. And, interestingly, his best performance as a Wildcat player came against none other than the Vols during his senior year of 1961-62.

"My best game was against the University of Tennessee," Pursiful smiled. "I'll be honest with you. I grew up in Bell County and I didn't like UT. We got the Tennessee newspapers and I had to read all that garbage about UK. If you check my stats against Tennessee, I had great games against them every game my senior year. I probably had the best game I had ever had at UK in the opening round of the UKIT against the University of Tennessee. I'll never forget it."

During the 1961-62 campaign, UK and Tennessee met three times, instead of the usual two-game home and away arrangement between both schools. And the Wildcats won all three meetings as the struggling Tennessee club completed the year with a dismal 4-19 mark, including 2-12 in SEC action. One of UK's victories over UT came in the University of Kentucky Invitational Tournament, where Pursiful poured in 34 points in a 96-69 victory. Also, he had 30 points against Tennessee in a 95-82 win at Knoxville.

At the end of Pursiful's senior year, Kentucky and fourth-rated Mississippi State shared SEC title with 13-1 marks. The 24-1 Bulldogs were guided by Babe McCarthy who later coached in the ABA with the New Orleans Buccaneers and the Kentucky Colonels. Because of its 49-44 victory over UK in Lexington earlier in the season, Mississippi State earned an automatic NCAA tourney berth as the league representative. But MSU turned down tourney because of the school's stand against racial integration. So Kentucky went to the big dance.

After an 81-60 victory over Butler in the Mideast Regional at Iowa City, UK advanced to meet top-ranked Ohio State and standouts Jerry Lucas and John Havlicek. Foul-plagued Kentucky, however, couldn't contain Lucas, who pumped in a game-high 33 points, as it lost by 10 points, a 74-64 verdict. The Wildcats had four players with four or more fouls, including two who went out with five fouls. According to Pursiful, who scored a team-high 21 points despite four fouls, it was the most disappointing moment of his UK career.

"That was the last game of my career and it was just a heartbreaking thing to end your career on a loss," Pursiful said. "My brother and sister-in-law were there and my parents couldn't get out there. But my parents came to every home game in Lexington. They didn't miss any home games."

Ohio State, coached by Fred Taylor, eventually went all the way to the 1962 Ohio-flavored NCAA championship game in Louisville, where the Buckeyes dropped to Cincinnati 71-59. It was Ohio State's third straight appearance in the Final Four, including the NCAA crown in 1960. (And Cincy was making its fourth consecutive appearance in the Final Four. In the following season of 1962-63, the Bearcats also advanced to the Final Four again, their fifth in five years.)

According to Pursiful, Lucas and Havlicek were the best players he had ever faced in addition to Jerry West of West Virginia. All three players were later elected to the Hall of Fame.

In his last year at UK, Pursiful — along with Cotton Nash — propelled the tradition-rich Wildcats back to their usual heights after a couple of so-called "down" years (18-7 and 19-9).

"We had less talent," said Pursiful, "but we had a sophomore All-American (in Nash) and he was great, probably one of the greatest players who has ever been at

Kentucky. The rest of us were just country boys and we just plodded along, worked hard and took a lot of pride in UK. We just meshed together as a team."

Some of the other key players on that team included 6-4 swingman Carroll Burchett, 6-0 Scotty Baesler, 6-4 Roy Roberts and 6-5 Allen Feldhaus, among others. "We were all very close, the players I played with," Pursiful commented. "We didn't have a lot of ability but we got along well and played as a team. I was probably closer to three people — Allen Feldhaus, Carroll Burchett and Scotty Baesler — because we roomed together. We roomed together all four years. We got to know each other's habits and thoughts. We really became pretty close. You know, with Scotty in Washington, D.C., and Feldhaus in Maysville, we see each other maybe once or twice a year."

Pursiful said he isn't surprised that Baesler got involved in poltics. A democrat farmer, Baesler is serving in the U.S. Congress as Kentucky's Sixth District representative. "His lifetime's ambition was to be governor one day," he said. "I knew he was into politics and I knew he would go far. Scotty is ambitious and a very talented individual."

Pursiful is deeply disturbed about the way the media has treated Rupp, who died in 1977, in recent years.

"I don't know all of the stories on coach Rupp, but I know that he was very similar to Bobby Knight," said Pursiful, who now lives in Louisville. "He was a perfectionist. He expected you to perform to perfection and I know that. I had no trouble with that.

"Of course, the media sometimes say he was a racist. When I played, the SEC schools did not have any blacks. They wouldn't play anyone who did (have blacks on the team) but we played anyone. Kentucky played Temple (with Guy Rodgers) and Notre Dame with Tommy

Hawkins (in the late 1950s), and all those great black players. He never gave any indication to us (that he was a racist)."

UK's well-publicized scandal in the late 1980s also troubled Pursiful. For various rules violations, the NCAA placed the school on a severe probation with one year of no live television and two years of no post-season tournament action.

"The recruiting scandal really bothered me because there is no reason for UK to have to do that," he said. "We can get the players without having to pay people to come there and play. Anytime there is negative publicity about UK, it bothers me because I took pride in playing for UK and I want it to be a first-class institution now. You got to take that with a grain of salt sometimes."

"I feel that they (NCAA) were tougher than they had been on a lot of other schools. I felt like they should-n't have been that harsh. I was hurt by all that went on because I didn't feel we needed to do that to get players. It was really disappointing to me."

In 1985, the *Lexington Herald-Leader* ran a series of controversial articles about the UK roundball program and college athletics. Many former Wildcat performers were quoted in the stories about payoffs from the boosters, among other items frowned upon by the NCAA.

"I wasn't surprised that the paper did that," Pursiful said. "I was mostly surprised that the players talked as much as they did. I never did understand that. Of course, some of them said they were misquoted and all that.

"One of the things coach Rupp preached was, 'Don't do anything to embarrass the university,' and you had to appreciate that. I would never have done anything to cause embarrassment."

During his college days, Pursiful met his future wife, Pris, at a church. "My brother, Darrell, was coaching down at Meade County High School (as an assistant) and I used to go visit him when I was in college," he said. "She went to the same church that he did." They have a grown daughter.

After spending some time at Phillips Petroleum Co., Pursiful entered the coaching profession. He went to Hodgenville where he was the head coach at LaRue County High School for several years.

His best year as a coach took place in 1971-72 when LaRue posted a 22-12 mark, according to Pursiful. But he "never made the state tournament as a coach or a player," said Pursiful. "I always dreamed of doing that and would have liked to do it."

In the spring of 1972, Joe B. Hall, the newly-named UK coach who replaced Rupp, visited Pursiful in Hodgenville. "The day he signed the contract at UK, he spoke at my basketball banquet at LaRue County," Pursiful said. "I was a personal friend of Joe Hall. I played for Joe on his team in the 1964 Olympic Trials. I know Joe very well.

"(For Hall), it was very difficult to go in there (UK basketball program) and follow a legend like Rupp. He got a lot of undue criticism. If you look at his record, he won about 20 games every year."

While coaching in Hodgenville, Pursiful was very active in a local Baptist church. And many years later, he was called to the ministry. He currently serves as the minister of activities at Carlisle Avenue Baptist Church in Louisville.

"God called me to the ministry when I was 47 years old," said the ex-Wildcat. "I didn't really want to go into the ministry. I had a business and was helping my wife run the business — a shoe store in Elizabethtown. I was attending church, singing in the choir and teaching Sunday School. I thought I was doing everything He wanted me to do, but He had other ideas."

Call him a Wildcat minister.

5 Big Jim
JIM ANDREWS

When the 1970-71 campaign began, Jim Andrews' main competition for playing time at Kentucky was 7-0 sophomore Tom Payne and 6-8 junior Mark Soderberg. Andrews was a promising 6-11 sophomore center, who was recruited out of Lima, Ohio, by assistant coach Joe B. Hall.

But after Soderberg, the Huntington Beach (Calif.) native who was Payne's primary backup, left the Wildcats in the early part of the season, Andrews saw his playing time gradually increase. He became more visible. It was now between Payne and Andrews. But Payne, whom everybody was watching very closely as he was the first black to play on UK's varsity team, dominated on the hardwood floor, leading the Wildcats to a 22-6 mark and earning first-team All-SEC honors.

Payne — the Louisville Shawnee High product who departed UK after his sophomore year to play with NBA's Atlanta Hawks — was not an easy teammate to play with, according to Andrews. Payne and Andrews only played together for one season as the former did not play on Kentucky's 1969-70 freshman squad for academic reasons. (Payne played for the Lexington AAU squad during his frosh year.)

"Tom was real full of himself," recalled Andrews. "As a freshman in high school, he didn't even make the basketball team. He barely made it as a sophomore. He didn't really start playing until he was a junior in high school. Being the first scholarship black at UK for basketball, I think, did something to his ego. The thing that Tom had at that time was just an overall lack of maturity. He was sometimes very difficult to deal with. He wanted his way all the time. He pouted and threw tantrums when things didn't go his way.

"I know one time we were playing Alabama and things weren't going his way. We were getting ready to eat a meal and he fell over into his plate. It was Jello, cake or something but he had it all over his face. We were all laughing and we took him back to his room. Nobody knew what was going on.

"Adolph (Rupp) made the decision that Tom wasn't going to start that night. I got to start and played a lot in that game. Tom wasn't much of a problem from that night on. Adolph would call your bluff. You might stand up to him once or maybe twice but not the third time."

Because of Payne, Andrews felt like he lost one year of valuable experience during his sophomore year.

When UK recruited Andrews, it didn't have any plans to sign Payne. While high-scoring star Dan Issel was bombing the SEC with his superb shooting, along with LSU's Pete Maravich, Kentucky looked for someone to fill in Issel's shoes. And with the help of then-current UK players Mike Pratt and Bob McCowan (both natives of Dayton, Ohio) and the Wildcat faithful living in the Dayton area, the Wildcats found Andrews and liked his roundball potential.

As a highly-regarded senior at Bath High School, Andrews led his team to an impressive 18-1 record, averaging 33 points and 18 rebounds a game. As a big man, Andrews was UK's future. At that time, the coaching staff had envisioned Andrews as the top center at Kentucky, not Payne who later entered UK's picture practically on his own.

"Joe (Hall) recruited me when Dan Issel was here," Andrews said. "Dan was going to be a senior and I was (going to be) a freshman. I was recruited as the No. 1 center to come in.

"What upset me was that Tom Payne signed a letter of intent (in the early summer of 1969) to come to UK and I talked to Joe about that. Joe had indicated two things to me. One is that they did not actively recruit Tom. Tom made the decision himself to come to Kentucky. Louisville did not have a national program at that time so he did not want to stay in Louisville.

"The other was that Joe did not think that Tom could make it academically so he was probably not going to be here at the university. A lot of things happened that he did get eligible.

"I felt that I lost one valuable year, my sophomore year, of playing time. Day in and day out I played better than Tom a number of times and I deserved to have some playing time."

Hall even went at lengths to discuss Andrews' unhappiness about the situation with Rupp. And the assistant thought both Andrews and Payne could function together at the same time.

"Joe had gone to Adolph many times and tried to convince him that we both should play at the same time," Andrews said. "I think it would have been a very good thing, a smart move. Later (Rick) Robey and (Mike) Phillips were the first (the so-called twin towers) to play at the same time."

Interestingly, Andrews didn't have any contact with Rupp — the head coach — until he signed a letter-of-intent with Kentucky at the high school. And it was by telephone when the player first talked to Rupp.

"He called to congratulate me and to welcome me

on board," Andrews said. "Joe did all of the recruiting and at that time the school was allowed to use local people, the alumni, to write letters and to visit. A lot of that went on. A very well-lubricated and -oiled machine was in place to recruit kids especially in the Ohio and the Dayton area. Mike Pratt, Bob McCowan and people from that area were instrumental in bringing me along with Dan Perry and Steve Penhorwood (who were also from Lima)."

And Rupp made an appearance at Andrews' high school awards dinner. Andrews said that itself was quite an experience that he'll always cherish.

"The first time that I met Rupp was when he flew in and spoke at my high school awards banquet with probably 100 or 150 people present," Andrews said. "I'll never forget (the moment when) he walked in and they applauded. Everybody knew who he was. This was after I signed with Kentucky."

Rupp was not the only coach that Andrews respected during the recruiting process. He also liked someone from Tennessee. His name was Ray Mears, the controversial head basketball coach for the Volunteers. So, had Kentucky not shown any interest in the player, he would've gone to UT. And the Vols wouldn't have been a bad choice. UT, led by senior All-American guard Bill Justus, had completed its outstanding 21-7 campaign in 1968-69 with a third-place finish in the NIT (which was considerably more important back then than it is now since the NCAA formerly invited only one representative from each league).

"I really admired Ray Mears as a person, as a basketball coach with what he was doing with the program at the University of Tennessee," said Andrews, whose parents divorced when he was about 10. "Ray Mears came to Lima, Ohio, and we went out and had dinner. We had an one-on-one conversation and he told me what his philosophy was and what he wanted to accomplish. It wasn't anything that I would call extraordinary.

"I ultimately decided against Tennessee because of the style of play. I talked to Ray Mears a number of times and he said he would have changed the way he played if he'd had a center that could run and shoot like I did. He said, 'I can't run with a team like Kentucky. With you, I would have changed my style.'

"I don't know if it would have happened or not but knowing how serious he was, it might have. Tennessee was my second choice. I was recruited by a lot of other schools — Ohio State, UCLA, Houston. UCLA was just too damn far. I just dropped it. I did not like the head coach for Ohio State at the time, Fred Taylor. He was, without a doubt, the most arrogant man I had ever met in my life. It was 1960 when they won the NCAA, but I think the talent carried him. History proved out; he'd never put together a program like that."

So UK won out the recruiting sweepstakes. The school had more to offer. Andrews liked its playing style, basketball tradition and the location. From Andrews' home in Ohio, Lexington was also a much shorter drive — by three hours — than Knoxville.

"Kentucky just kind of matched up for me," said Andrews, who once poured in a last-second shot in 1972 as host UK edged Mears and UT 72-70. "They matched with how I liked to play, a small town and tremendous support for the program. It was a case if I get my degree from the University of Kentucky, would I want to live here (in Lexington) the rest of my life? My answer was yes. I had no desire to live in Ohio, no desire to live in Houston. Knoxville would have been nice, but at that time I wouldn't have wanted to be in Knoxville, either. Kentucky was close to my family, many of whom live in West Virginia. In fact, I thought about West Virginia, but it just wasn't a very good college program."

Andrews went through the Wildcat program for three years, including his freshman season, under Rupp's leadership before the Baron's forced retirement in 1972. They saw a lot of each other. The ailing Rupp, however, sometimes got upset with Andrews, whom he thought was kind of lazy. The coach believed the player didn't try hard enough.

"I did things pretty much at my speed," Andrews admitted. "It wasn't that I was hard-headed or a problem. There were some days that I didn't feel like playing so I just didn't do it. I would listen to what he said versus how he said it. I would think what I thought he meant and I don't want to do it and I didn't. I paid for it once in a while. He wanted me to be more active and involved in the game so he said I was lazy. That really wasn't very true. The thing that Adolph Rupp didn't understand about me was that the psychology he used on other players didn't work on me."

During his junior year — Rupp's last season at UK — All-SEC center Andrews paced the 1971-72 Wildcats in scoring and rebounding. He averaged 21.5 points and 11.3 rebounds. His teammate, 6-7 senior Tom Parker, was chosen the SEC Player of the Year by the Associated Press. And the SEC co-champion Wildcats finished the year with a 21-7 worksheet after going 1-1 in the NCAA tournament, beating coach Al McGuire and Marquette 85-69 and dropping to coach Hugh Durham and Florida State 73-54. (Florida State eventually advanced to the NCAA championship game before losing to 6-11 Bill Walton and his unbeaten UCLA gang 81-76.)

It was a very difficult year for Andrews and his teammates. The 70-year-old Rupp, who was fighting to keep his job despite a mandatory retirement rule, had three assistants on his coaching staff — Joe B. Hall, Gale Catlett and Dick Parsons. His aides, especially Hall and

Catlett, sometimes told the players what to do at the same time, acting like the head coach. The players became confused many times and the NCAA tourney loss to 10th-ranked Florida State in Dayton, Ohio, served as an example.

"The thing that I remember most about that game was total confusion," Andrews said. "At that time, it was potentially Rupp's last ballgame and he wanted Gale Catlett, one of his pets, to be his successor but Joe (Hall) had the inside track. The players really didn't want Gale, a nice guy. His style wasn't the Kentucky style. There was so much confusion and politicking with the coaches and the players. I think Dick Parsons, not that he wanted to be head coach, wanted to remain with the program. If Joe was the inside guy, that's where his loyalty was.

"During that game I can't stress how much confusion there was. We had a timeout and I had three different sets of instructions on how to play defense on players. It got so bad that we didn't know who to listen to. At one timeout, we just asked them, 'Who are we going to listen to?' Obviously, Rupp said, 'It's me.'

"Florida State was playing the game of their lives so it's a wonder we didn't get beat more than we did. It was just totally confusing. We didn't know who to listen to or where to play. Just two nights before, we played Marquette, a nationally-ranked team, and we beat them fairly handy. According to *Sports Illustrated* and the media, Marquette was supposed to blow us off the floor. It just didn't happen and if we had won that ballgame (against Florida State), we'd be in the Final Four. I think it was obvious even to the fans that we didn't know where to go or who to listen to.

"I think Rupp, in his heart, still thought he would stay on. (Former Kentucky Gov.) Happy Chandler was doing all he could do and others as well."

What did Rupp say to the team after his last game?

"He came in and said his normal thing after a loss," Andrews said. "At that point, he hadn't given up. He thought he was coming back for another year. There was still some doubt about whether he was going to be forced to retire or not."

The Rupp era later came to an end when UK announced that Hall would be the school's next head basketball coach. That didn't suit many folks very well, making the situation awkward for the new mentor and the Wildcats as the 1972-73 season approached. But the coaching change didn't bother Andrews very much as he grew up in another state.

"I was recruited from out of state so it really didn't matter to me," Andrews said. "I played at three different high schools for four different basketball coaches. To me, a coach was a coach, one more instrument to accomplish what I wanted to do. I didn't see the forced retirement of Rupp in 1972 any differently than if anybody else came in and took over the job.

"I think for some players, it may have (bothered them). For the players, who were from Kentucky and grew up with Kentucky basketball, it probably was (difficult)."

In Hall's first year as the UK boss, the Wildcats did fairly well, capturing the SEC title and winning 20 games against eight losses. An honorary captain, Andrews led the team — loaded with promising sophomores such as Kevin Grevey, Jimmy Dan Conner, Mike Flynn and Bob Guyette — in scoring with a 20.1-point average. Andrews, who was also the Wildcats' top rebounder with 12.4 rebounds, received All-SEC honors for the second year in a row.

But it wasn't a very smooth season for senior Andrews and the Wildcat program, which didn't have Rupp as the coach for the first time since 1930. Hall's Wildcats didn't get off to a good start. After winning the season opener against Michigan State on the road, they suffered three straight losses, including a 78-70 setback to Dean Smith's North Carolina squad at Louisville when a frustrated Hall stormed the Freedom Hall floor in protest of the officials. The downhearted Wildcat faithful began to doubt Hall's coaching ability as UK's record dipped to 1-3. The folks wondered if UK perhaps had made a big mistake in coercing Rupp to retire.

But the Wildcats regrouped and won seven of the next eight games en route to the NCAA tournament. UK's future began to look brighter. Hall, in the meantime, attempted to welcome a bitter Rupp — who sometimes criticized the squad on his television show — back to the program. Hall invited the former coach to the practice at Memorial Coliseum and participate.

"He (Rupp) didn't come much at all in the beginning," Andrews said. "Joe went out of his way to go get him and let him know he was important. (Hall) set him down and let him talk to us. I think Adolph appreciated that. We've got two monuments to Rupp: Memorial Coliseum — the House That Rupp Built and Rupp Arena. Now there is a museum so he's still very much alive in the program, some 18 years after his death."

During the early stage of his UK coaching career, Hall was uptight. Especially his first year. He tried very hard to please the fans showing that he could do the job as he was the man who replaced the legend. Hall wanted to be successful.

"When Joe took over the program, there was a certain amount of pressure to succeed Rupp," Andrews said. "Adolph did not dislike Joe. It was that he did not want to retire. He was someone who would have liked to die on the bench or at least picked his time to retire. He was in poor health. He had problems with diabetes and he had lost part of his foot — a couple of toes. Finally, that last year he went to the (state) legislature and appealed the mandatory retirement rule. That was turned down. Joe had to replace him and Adolph didn't make it real easy.

"Joe and I talked about it a number of times and we had an understanding that I would listen to what he had to say. Joe was the coach. Adolph always had the loyalty of his players and when he left we were loyal to the coach, Joe Hall. It was hard for Adolph to face and understand that. He made it difficult for us. It could have been a lot smoother.

"The pressure was so great that Joe would say things during the timeouts that made little sense. I would go back the next day to talk to him about it and he would-n't remember. The pressure so intense that he would lit-erally explode and say things he didn't recall. A lot of that pressure was self-induced. It was the competitive spirit in Joe.

"But in the last few years that he coached, (Hall changed his methods). He said, 'I'm different to what I was when I had you boys. I've learned to relax and enjoy the game and not take it so seriously.' I think those were the years that he did his best coaching. That was after he won the (national) championship in 1978. He enjoyed the game more after he had proven his point."

Having played for both Rupp and Hall, Andrews said there were differences in their coaching styles. In all of Andrews' three varsity seasons, the Wildcats won or shared SEC championships.

On Rupp: "He was a student of psychology. He had a way of evaluating talent. People responded to what he wanted to do. Playing under Adolph, there were five posi-tions and that was it. If you weren't one of the five, then you did not play very much. There were some exceptions — maybe if you were a sixth man. You had to try to become part of the team during the offseason. He was very good at keeping track of which kids were working or what you were doing.

"Adolph wasn't concerned with curfews that much. If some of his players were going to break the rules, he did-n't want to know about it. He was one of those fellows (who felt) no news is good news. He stayed away from it."

On Hall: "Joe was more concerned with rules and curfews. Joe relied a lot on technique and less on psycho-logical motivation the first couple of years. Adolph probably wrote the book on a lot of things that were done and Joe was more of a student at that time. He studied other coaching and teaching methods. He spent a great deal of time working in clinics with other coaches so he would understand it. He would adapt very well. From that time on, Joe was much of a motivator.

"Joe had conditioning and weight programs. All the other coaches had to do the same thing in order to catch up. That was another part of Joe using strategy and technique to recruit good players and I thought he was excellent at that. Joe was one of the great recruiters with the best eye for talent that I ever associated with. He had a way of looking at the kid as an athlete but also as a student and a well-rounded person."

Did Andrews break any team rules?

"I can't remember," he laughed. "You might have to ask Joe that. I can remember a couple of players being caught. I think I broke a curfew a couple of times but I wasn't caught. We did a good job covering for each other."

There was one incident when Andrews made up an excuse for his roommate Larry Stamper, a 6-6 forward who was out visiting his girlfriend late at night. Doing his regular checkup duties on the players, Hall visited their room and asked where Stamper was.

"I think he's doing laundry," said a nervous Andrews, who actually knew his roommate was at girl-friend's place.

So Andrews rushed to the car and drove five minutes to get his roommate back to their room. "We came back in and got a basket of laundry and he didn't get into any trouble," recalled Andrews. "Whether coach Hall believed that or not, I don't know but that was our story. I also remember as soon as Joe left, Larry went back out."

In 1973, two professional basketball teams selected Andrews. At that time, pro basketball had two rival leagues — the older, established National Basketball Association and the younger, promising American Basketball Association. The NBA's Seattle SuperSonics drafted Andrews in the seventh round, while the Indiana Pacers of the ABA picked the ex-Wildcat, also in the seventh round. Seattle, coming off a horrible 26-56 season under two different coaches, named NBA great Bill Russell as its new head coach for the upcoming campaign. Indiana, meanwhile, was one of the ABA's better franchises.

But things didn't work out for Andrews, who later flew to Italy to play pro basketball. He didn't like what he saw at both places. Indiana had financial difficulties and Seattle had Russell, a 6-9 black who supposedly didn't care for any "white" rookies.

"That year there was serious consideration they (the Pacers) were going to disband," Andrews explained. "They had just won the ABA (for the second straight time in 1973, beating the Kentucky Colonels). They traded many players and waived every rookie that year. They just kept a handful of players. The contract we had negotiated with Indiana was $28,000 a year and $10,000 a year whether I made the team or not. They never did pay me the bonus. They were broke. For almost six weeks, nobody was paid."

Meanwhile, the Seattle management called Andrews and asked him to try out with the SuperSonics. But Russell said not to bother even though Andrews and the NBA club had discussed contractual terms, which was basically the same as Indiana's.

"Bill Russell was very much a civil rights activist at that time," Andrews commented. "He was making up for the wrongs done against blacks and his team was mostly black. My being 6-11 and white did not fit into his plans. I talked to a lot of players and we all agreed that he would make my life absolutely miserable."

So Andrews ended up in Europe, playing pro basketball for three years. His temporary home was at Naples, a large city in southern Italy.

"When I played, the players were not paid anything like they are today," said Andrews, who once grew up in a home without indoor plumbing. "In the ABA, the players averaged $20,000 to 25,000 a year. The NBA wasn't much better. Playing in Europe, you were paid more than you were in the United States. All that money in Europe was tax-free. If you had a $30,000-a-year contract, it was like $60,000 here. There were a lot of other perks: cars, eating and a place to live. It was very comfortable. Their sports figures are very revered."

After Italy, he also spent some time in Sweden. But he encountered problems, especially financial, in the northern European country.

The money-hungry entrepreneurs "wanted to start a league in Sweden," Andrews said. "Sweden was a socialist country and a lot of the managers were corrupt. They took all the money. We were supposed to be flying to other locations but we would have to drive our own cars, maybe take trains, and pay our own way. These people were putting money in their pockets. It was the only way they could become wealthy. There was an income cap in Sweden and after so many dollars you gave everything you earned back to the government."

A more mature Andrews returned to the UK campus for the 1976-77 academic season. Several hours short of his degree requirements when he left school three years earlier, he wanted to complete his education and graduate. Also, at the same time, he would coach the Wildcats as a graduate assistant under Joe B. Hall. Coming off an NIT championship season, Kentucky was preparing to move to brand-new Rupp Arena with senior Larry Johnson and juniors Jack Givens, James Lee, Rick Robey and Mike Phillips

"I was a few hours short and also wanted to look at different careers that I might want to take and basketball was one of them," said Andrews, who received his degree in general studies with history and geography. "They were paying for my tuition. They owed that to me because you were given a five-year scholarship. I didn't use all of my original (allotment) so when I came back I took advantage to use the rest of it.

"At first (then-AD) Cliff Hagan didn't want to go along with it but Joe said he wanted every one of his players to graduate. I think up to that point every player but one had graduated."

Earlier, when Andrews first came to UK, he majored in chemistry. But his advisors told him that he couldn't do it because of basketball and he therefore changed his major to physical education. He eventually changed it to history and had ambitious thoughts about becoming a lawyer. However, after talking to a couple of former Wildcat players, he changed his mind about a possible law career.

"I went into history and thought I wanted to go into pre-law," he said, "but Scotty Baesler said there was no money and hours are terrible. I talked to John Adams, too. He was traveling down to London, doing district work. He said it was hard."

In his second stint at UK, Andrews didn't stay long. He only coached the Wildcats for one year. The reason was financial and he had a family to support.

Andrews commented, "Joe wanted me to come back, but I said, 'No thank you and I'm going to find another career. I'll come back to basketball when I can afford it.' We kind of left it at that. Joe was making good money but it wasn't the kind coaches make today. Coaches today make half a million to a million dollars for a Division I school. It's a tremendous amount of money.

"The money was terrible. I think that I was paid like $250 a month. There was no family or home life at all. I couldn't imagine becoming a full-time assistant with all that travel and so on."

And he moved on to a successful career in business and later earned his MBA degree from Xavier University in Cincinnati, Ohio.

Andrews and his second wife, Julie, whom he married in 1984, are proud of Julie Beth Hayden's accomplishments. Hayden, who is Andrews' stepdaughter, is profoundly deaf. Now in her early twenties, she has overcome many obstacles in becoming a successful citizen in the hearing world through hard work and family support. She even went to the same university where her stepdad starred in basketball over two decades ago. Hayden uses the oral mode of communication (lip reading) as well as sign language.

Andrews was involved in the Louisville Deaf Oral School in 1978 when he met his future wife and her daughter. The mother was active at the school through PTA. "I got to met her daughter, Julie Beth, at that time," he said. "My interest was not in the mother. My interest was in the daughter. And, in 1982, I was having problems with my (first) marriage and got divorced. We talked and ended up getting married. We got married in Louisville."

The ex-UK star also has a teenage son, Michael, by a previous marriage.

In the fall of 1985, just as new basketball coach Eddie Sutton prepared his first season at Kentucky, the *Lexington Herald-Leader* published highly-controversial stories about the ex-Wildcat players, among others, accepting gifts from boosters in apparent violation of NCAA rules. Understandably, many folks, including Andrews, were outraged.

"I know they won the Pulitzer Prize," Andrews in an 1986 interview with the author which appeared in the *Commonwealth Journal* in Somerset and *The Cats' Pause*. "But I thought it was junk. It didn't accomplish anything, because we're talking about things that happened years ago. I think what they should have done was look at, say, 15 or 20 schools — not just one — and talk about what goes on in each one of those recruiting programs. I think they would have had something very good, if they'd done that."

Asked if he felt the Lexington newspaper had used some journalism tricks in getting those stories, Andrews replied, "Yes, a lot of them. But I'm not going to give any examples, mainly because I think that would be trying to get back at them. What's done is done. I think they should look at what they have done to some people, though. Some people have been libeled and can't get jobs today, because of what they wrote. Some of the things they wrote were true, but others were taken out of context...."

And Andrews, in an 1994 interview, has some observations about today's news media. "I think there are two things that have happened. The players today are taught how to respond. The media has to do a better job. They aren't tougher; they just do a better job than 20 years ago. Access to the locker rooms and to the players were tougher back then and today it happens two or three times a week. It is a constant flood of information. Most of it is just not worthwhile. Most of it is tabloid. I always thought the media should stick to the story. You need to be aware of things, but a lot is media hype."

Like most people, Andrews was initially amazed that New Yorker Rick Pitino would leave his home for the Bluegrass in 1989 to guide the Wildcats.

"I was surprised he would leave New York," he said. "He is the embodiment of New York. He loves it. He loves the area and the ability to be a big fish in a big pond as opposed to a big fish in a little pond here. He has the ability to market himself and manipulate the media. With all those trappings, I was surprised that he would come here to this program.

"After I got to know him and talk to him, it doesn't surprise me because he enjoys the college program. If it doesn't have the potential to be first class, then he isn't interested. Knowing that about him now, I can see why he came here to this program. I think a lot of that is due to (former UK star and ex-New York Knicks player) Kenny Walker talking about how good Lexington is."

On occasional rumors about Pitino leaving Kentucky for NBA, Andrews said, "You can't do anything about rumors. I don't worry about anything until it happens. Worry is a negative thing. Here in Lexington there isn't a lot for the media to write about. So if you write about something, you have to hunt the negative."

6 "Oh Honey, Your Hair Is Too Long...."

DOUG FLYNN

When the 5-10, 155-pound Doug Flynn first showed up at UK's freshman team practice at Memorial Coliseum, a 6-6, 200-pound rookie by the name of Larry Stamper approached the pint-sized guard.

"Get me a glass of water," Stamper said.

"What do I look like — the towel boy?" Flynn snapped back.

"Yeah, that's what you look like," said the big freshman.

And Stamper sheepishly found out that the "towel boy" turned out to be a scholarship player. "He couldn't believe it," Flynn said later.

That was in the fall of 1969. At that time, the highly-regarded Wildcats had 6-9 high-scoring senior Dan Issel, who was coming off a remarkable campaign as All-American junior. But Flynn or Stamper couldn't play for the varsity team. Unlike today's rookies, freshmen were not eligible for the varsity competition back then.

But Flynn, a three-sport product out of Lexington Bryan Station High School, and the other freshmen actively participated in the UK roundball program. They practiced with the varsity as well as playing on a regular freshman schedule.

"It was a thrill to go on the floor each day with the No. 1 team in the nation," recalled Flynn, who stayed at UK for only one season before eventually moving on as a veteran major league baseball player. "We would go early and play against them every day. It was a learning experience for me because it helped me to grow up a little bit. The year was phenomenal. I was around Adolph Rupp. Adolph was still coach of the varsity. Joe Hall was the coach of the freshman team, along with Dickie Parsons.

"I got beat up pretty good just because it was a very physical game. I was so small that I just tried to survive. The guys all treated me extremely well. I still have friendships with an awful lot of them. I remember Dan Issel, even though he was a superstar, sneaking us an extra hamburger or two when we went on the road. He was that way to everybody and still is."

The varsity Wildcats finished one of their most memorable seasons in school history with a sparkling 26-2 mark and No. 1 national ranking. The Wildcats' hopes for a national championship were shattered in the NCAA Mideast Regional tourney in Columbus, Ohio, when 7-2 giant Artis Gilmore and his Jacksonville teammates stunned UK 106-100 in a high-scoring affair. It was Rupp's last great team at Kentucky.

Despite his size, Flynn started every game for UK's 1969-70 freshman team, which had five scholarship rookies. In addition to Flynn, the other scholarship players were 6-11 Jim Andrews, 6-4 Steve Penhorwood, 6-8 Dan Perry and Stamper. The freshman games were usually played as preliminaries to the varsity matchups.

"There were some really goofy things that happened," Flynn said of his days as a freshman. "We went to one game at Tennessee and they had a rule that the varsity had to have a certain amount of time to warm up (before its game began). So what the officials would do if they were running out of time, they would set the clock at five minutes and just let it run down. We lost two games in the last seconds because the other team would let the clock run down. They (opponents) would go to the free throw line, and instead of taking 10 seconds to shoot, they would take 30.

"I know that we lost one game in Dayton where all five of us fouled out. We were up, rolling and playing good. Then we were all on the bench with fouls. I used to tease my dad (Bobby) who was a University of Dayton grad that I now knew why they (the Flyers) won so many games up there."

The Kittens, guided by first-year head freshman coach Joe B. Hall, finished with a 16-6 mark.

There was a player who was not eligible to participate on the freshman squad for academic reasons. The player's name was 7-0 Tom Payne, who later made history as the first black to play for the varsity Wildcats. After making the grades as a frosh, Payne received a basketball scholarship.

But UK also had another black, Darryl Bishop. He played on the freshman team. A 6-3, 200-pounder from Louisville Seneca High, Bishop actually became the first black to play either on the freshman or varsity basketball team at Kentucky. He made his frosh debut in a win over Cincinnati at Memorial Coliseum, scoring 16 points. Freshman teammate Jim Andrews added 31 points in the victory.

"I roomed with the first to ever play there — Darryl Bishop," commented Flynn, who scored 13 points in that frosh game with Cincy. "Tom was ineligible so Darryl was there (as the first black to play roundball at UK). Darryl and I were good friends." Actually, Bishop was on a football scholarship and later made All-SEC defensive back in 1972 and '73 under coaches John Ray and Fran Curci.

On Feb. 21, 1970, Flynn found out, more or less, what a true friend he had in Bishop when UK and LSU had a doubleheader — the freshman and varsity games. The varsity game, featuring the top-ranked Wildcats and the nation's top scorer in LSU's Pete Maravich, was being regionally televised in the South.

But the early-bird fans who watched the freshman game certainly got their money's worth as Flynn got involved in an ugly confrontation with a LSU freshman. Consequently, the officials ejected Flynn from the game.

"That day we had a full house and I was having a pretty good game and I ended up getting in a fight," Flynn said. "This guy hit me and I hit him back. I remember Joe Hall grabbing me and pulling me off the guy. I happened to hit him pretty good and he went down. The next thing that I knew Joe had a hold on me, and Darryl Bishop was sitting on the guy and had him pinned down and was hitting him pretty good. He took up for me because we were roommates. There were not very many blacks in the whole gym at all."

But Rupp, who was watching as an interested observer, didn't like the scene, at least from the public standpoint. In Kentucky's dressing room during the half-time, "He chewed me out pretty good," Flynn said. "He said that I was an embarrassment to the university, I was an embarrassment to the state of Kentucky. Then he made me walk back out on the floor in front of all those people and sit and watch the rest of the game from there. As I walked out, they got on me pretty good."

Later, Issel visited Flynn in his motel room and offered some advice as the Wildcats stayed overnight during a two-game road trip against LSU and Alabama.

"You okay?" Issel wondered.

"I'm fine," said Flynn.

"When you are having a good game like that, you have to do everything that you can to stay on the floor. Especially since you are the ball handler on this team and you are the one who brings the ball up the floor."

"Yeah," said Flynn, "but what about coach Rupp?"

"Coach Rupp loved it. He wished that everybody had that kind of fight," Issel smiled.

On his roommate, Flynn remembers the day Bishop arrived on the campus. "When he got here, I remember them (the staff) asking, 'Would you mind rooming with him?' That was nothing for me to do. Color never meant a thing to me. I remember my dad being the only white on an all-black baseball team in Lexington. (Race) was never even an issue to me. Darryl and I became good friends. After that I went on and he stayed. He played a little more basketball and football. I think that he ended up getting into a little bit of trouble with Elmore Stephens."

Later, during the 1971-72 season, Bishop played varsity basketball when he, along with football player Elmore Stephens, walked on, helping the struggling Wildcats who were short of players. But Rupp dropped both walk-ons from the squad for missing a road trip.

When Flynn played freshman basketball, the SEC had several black players such as Wendell Hudson of Alabama and Henry Harris of Auburn. Flynn said he didn't believe Bishop encountered any racial hardships at UK. "I don't ever remember Darryl going through that much trouble," Flynn said. "Maybe I wasn't aware of it that much. He didn't say anything to me. He got treated real good at Kentucky. Darryl was a good guy so you had no reason to treat him bad. I didn't see Tom Payne because I wasn't around him much."

When Rupp first saw Flynn at a practice, he didn't recognize or know the youngster. The freshmen were scrimmaging against the varsity. At one point when Flynn hit three straight shots against the varsity players, Rupp screamed and stopped the play.

"Are you that kid from Lafayette?" said Rupp, who had thought Flynn was the other kid who had signed with UK.

"No," replied a nervous Flynn, who noticed that Issel and other players were laughing.

"Who the hell is he, Harry?" yelled Rupp, turning to his assistant, Harry Lancaster (who eventually left the coaching ranks to concentrate on his UK athletic director post.)

Before Lancaster had a chance to respond, Rupp turned to Joe Hall, "Who is he, Joe?"

Looking back, Flynn said, "He (Rupp) had no idea who I was. It is kind of funny because that was the first time I ever confronted Adolph Rupp."

The other confrontation with Rupp was later at LSU when Flynn became involved in a brawl.

Originally, UK didn't have any plans for Flynn. But in the late summer of 1969, Kentucky changed its mind and contacted Flynn after one of its freshman basketball recruits had signed a minor league baseball contract.

"I was looking at a few junior collges and I got a phone call," Flynn said. "They said they need a point guard for their freshman team. If you don't make it in basketball, we will guarantee you a baseball scholarship. So that is why I went to Kentucky. I didn't have any scholarship offers to go any place. I didn't make all-city teams but I liked to compete."

When Flynn arrived at UK, everyone told him that he was too small to play college basketball. At 5-10, you would think he would be the shortest player on the team. But that wasn't the case. The Kittens had 5-4, 145-pound guard John Gabbard on their roster.

"I had been small all of my life," said Flynn. "I was lucky to play for a good high school coach, Bobby Barlow. My dad was small and he had been a great competitor. I wasn't even the smallest on that team. I was used to hearing that from a lot of people. We had a walk-on by the name of John Paul Gabbard from Beattyville, who was a friend of Larry Stamper. He was very small, so he walked on. He was a good guy.

"Most of the guys that I had to guard my freshman year were 6-foot or bigger. It was a great learning experience because it taught survival. I look at things that (former Kentucky guard) Travis Ford did and getting someone to the free throw line, etc. You learn to play to survive and to win — grabbing people's trunks, hitting their elbow as they went up to shoot, eating garlic before a game. That was just part of the game. I'm glad that I was a little smaller. I think it helped me as far as being competitive. Basketball was good to me, especially being so small."

As it turned out, Flynn said he "had a pretty good freshman year and I won a leadership award although I really wasn't the best player. None of them (the other players) were floor leaders so I guess that's why they gave me the award."

Needless to say, Flynn — who also played baseball at UK in a reserve capacity — certainly had a big heart with a fighting spirit.

After his freshman year, Flynn received bad news. "I ended up not having the grades to stay at UK," he recalled.

But an embarrassed Flynn said he was a decent student and he had a gut feeling that the school wanted to remove him to make room for another scholarship.

"The problem was that I had study hall with all the players of which I attended every one," Flynn said. "I had classes with all the players. I studied very hard. Yet some of these guys, even though they didn't quite make it to class, seemed to be getting better grades than me.

"When I would ask to see my paper, they wouldn't show it to me. All I needed was one grade changed as it turned out. Actually, I never saw a paper and I always felt that I did a lot better. I went to a junior college, had a 3.67 (grade-point average) and I studied no more down there. Something fishy was up. They had a way of getting rid of you if they needed your scholarship. It was very embarrassing for me but it turned out to be the best thing that ever happened to me.

"(But) I wasn't too happy about the headlines saying that I flunked out of college because I knew better. It wasn't really the headlines because I was a nobody. It was just a normal thing in the paper. It was embarrassing because everyone who knew me knew what happened or at least thought they knew what happened."

So Flynn drove 75 miles south of Lexington and enrolled at UK's Somerset Community College for the 1970-71 season. He was set to play basketball for the SCC squad, coached by Bob Anderson, as a sophomore member.

However, he ended up playing only one game for SCC, scoring 15 points against the UK Dental School in a 102-87 setback. The squad from the Dental School had several players from the major college ranks, including ex-Wildcat players Jim LeMaster and Tom Porter, and former Vandy star Kenny Gibbs of Somerset. (Both LeMaster, who today is the president of the UK Basketball Museum, and Porter played on the famous Rupp's Runts squad.)

"We thought I could go there and play basketball," Flynn said. "I went through all the practices and played the first game (actually the second game of the season). Then NJCAA said that I was ineligibile to play. Because I was ineligible at UK, I was also ineligible there.

"I had grown a little bit when I went to Somerset. I had grown to 5-11 and up to about 165 pounds. I started to mature a little bit. I was finally getting a chance to score. At Kentucky, I didn't get a chance to shoot much. I had to give the ball off to the big guys. But I had matured a little bit and I was to be the scorer on that team. I liked that. And the people there treated me like a king. I have nothing but fond memories of the people of Somerset, Ky."

Even after he wasn't allowed to play basketball, Flynn continued his education at SCC. While taking some summer classes and playing slow-pitch softball in 1971, he attended a local baseball tryout camp sponsored by the Cincinnati Reds in Somerset. Actually, he and his buddies went to the camp for fun.

"Some friends of mine woke me up, gave me shoes and a glove as I didn't have any of the equipment with me," Flynn commented. "I went to the first camp and tried out. I had on a pair of shorts and maybe not even any socks but after I got there, I realized that I was as good as most everyone there. I started getting more serious."

It marked his very first step to the major leagues. The Reds liked Flynn's potential and they invited him to other camps in Frankfort and Lexington. Then he traveled to Cincinnati, his fourth tryout, for another chance.

"I went to Riverfront Stadium for another tryout," he said. "I started getting excited because I thought maybe this is what I want. But I wasn't sure since I had always wanted to play basketball. I felt like I was getting a little stronger and I was maturing. So, why not give it a shot for a little bit? And if I didn't make it, I could always come back home and finish up my college (degree)."

Flynn, 20 years old at the time, did make the cut. Cincinnati scout Chet Montgomery signed the youngster to a free agent pact with the Reds. "I didn't sign for very much money," he said. "I think it was about $2,500 or maybe $3,000. The money was primarily to pay for school. It wasn't much. I don't even remember spending it."

In 1972, during his first spring training with the Reds organization in Florida, Flynn played on a rookie league squad. He was one of the older players on the team. But he didn't stay in the rookie league very long.

"The third baseman in Class A ball got hurt so my manager asked me if I could play third base and I said, 'Sure, I played in high school,' which I never did," Flynn recalled. "And they moved me up to Class A ball."

The Reds assigned Flynn to the Tampa club of the Class A Florida State League. Russ Nixon, who later became the Reds manager in the 1980s, was Flynn's manager. In his first game with Tampa, Flynn played at third base.

But Flynn had problems. Nixon tried to position Flynn at third properly, yelling, "Back up, move in." The player, however, became confused.

"Come here! You never played third before?" said a suspicious Nixon.

"Nope," Flynn said.

"So, you lied."

"Well, I would have told you anything to move up the ladder."

And Flynn stayed with Tampa for the entire 1972 campaign. "Nixon liked me so I played a little bit the first year, not a whole lot, not every day," he said. "He told me that I would play every day some place next year and he has been a good friend of mine ever since."

In his first pro season, Flynn batted for a lowly .211 average in 98 games. He didn't set the world on fire. As far as hitting is concerned, he had a long way to go. But the Reds liked his fielding. They were hopeful about his potential.

Flynn began to move up in the Reds' minor league system as he showed promise at Three Rivers (Class AA) and Indianapolis (Class AAA) in 1973 and '74, respectively. Life in the minor leagues, for the most part, has never been rosy, but it certainly wasn't dull. "You meet a lot of wild men in the minors," Flynn said. "Most of them are right out of high school. When you have that many guys all trying to get to the same level, you will do almost anything to relax and let out some frustration."

Flynn made his major league debut with Cincinnati, popularly known as the Big Red Machine, in 1975. It was the year the Reds had captured the World Series, called by some the most exciting ever, in defeating the Boston Red Sox. The Reds, guided by manager Sparky Anderson, finished with a sparkling 108-54 mark in the regular season. *The Sporting News*, in 1989, ranked the 1975 Reds as the sixth best team in the entire baseball history, behind the top-rated New York Yankees of 1927.

As a backup infielder, Flynn didn't see much action. But he contributed enough to help the Reds win. For the year, he batted for a .268 average in 89 contests. Several of his teammates assisted the Lexington native in adjusting his new life as a major leaguer.

"Darrel Chaney, Bill Plummer — those guys really stick out in my mind — because they were very good to me," Flynn said. "Even though I was there to take Darrel Chaney's job away as an utility player, he still was very good to me. In fact, we are in business together in Fantasy Baseball camps today."

Cincinnati's Pete Rose, who currently holds major league baseball record for most career hits, was also cordial to Flynn. "Pete Rose was always very good to me," he said. "He was one of the big guys. I never said much. I just did as I was told and went out and tried to play hard. He always respected that so he has remained a good friend. I talked to Pete all the time. I played softball with him recently in Florida against singer Michael Bolton and others."

And Rose was the probably most interesting personality he has met in baseball, according to Flynn. "I won't explain all the reasons why," he said. "He was a walking baseball encyclopedia. I've never seen anybody that could concentrate so much and loved the game under adverse circumstances. He played hard every time that he played. He was kind of complex in that he did a lot of things that people didn't approve of. When he came to the ball park, there was nobody better. He got his divorce papers in New York and that day he got five hits (in 1979). He could separate personal from professional life. That's why he was so good. His concentration level was so good. I couldn't do it but that's why he was a superstar."

On his first major league salary of $16,500, Flynn said, "That was the minimum. Today, it is around $120,000. (The actual minimum figure today is $109,000.) It was good. You couldn't pay a whole lot of bills with it, but it was OK. You got meal money, which was separate, and you got licensing money which was about $1,000 at the time. You were in the big leagues and that was important. So you didn't care (about the pay). It was before the agents (came along) and I was happy with it. On that team in 1975, we had 15 guys making less than $30,000 a year. That is considered one of the best teams of all times — that team and the 1976 team. You know Cincinnati is very cheap and they've been very cheap for a lot of years."

In the following year of 1976, Flynn's baseball stock soared as the Reds (102-60) won their second straight World Series championship. He hit for a respectable .283 average in 93 games. When all-star second baseman Joe Morgan was injured in June, Flynn took over Morgan's spot and hit .418 in a 15-game stretch.

While at Cincinnati, Flynn did not spend much

time, if any, with Anderson, who later became the only manager to capture World Series titles in both leagues. "He didn't spend a lot of time with guys who weren't the stars," Flynn said. "He is known for that. That's not a secret. Sparky always hung out with the big guys. If you were one of the little guys, you did not expect to hang out with him. That was just Sparky. He was good with the fans, good with the superstars. If you were an extra person, he may not spend as much time with you.

"I didn't talk to him very much, but I was comfortable with the other guys and that was all that mattered. (Johnny) Bench, Rose, Morgan and (Tony) Perez were the heart of that team. You had the blacks, Latinos and the white guys playing together. You had role models for every group of people. They were the leaders of that ball club so you did as they did. There was never a problem."

Playing for the Reds certainly highlighted Flynn's career at the time. But he also had some personal problems to deal with at home after his second major league season.

In January of 1977, his 24-year-old sister, Melanie Flynn, disappeared in a bizarre incident. Her family has not seen her since and they are still searching for the truth. Melanie worked as a secretary at the Kentucky High School Athletic Association in Lexington.

Flynn said it hurts to read about his sister and the entire case in the newspapers. "Yeah, especially when you know that something should be done about it," he noted. "It's painful when the town you grew up in, the town you still live in, the town where you pay money (taxes), the town you try to do good and see that the people in this town covers it up. I'm really disappointed in the way it's been handled. I'm really disappointed that there haven't been people with some guts in downtown because they know what's happened. For 17 years or so, they have let it go by. When something happens and it is covered up, it is painful.

"It bothers my parents more. It affects all of us at this time. They've awakened my mom and when the red-head gets upset and starts on a mission, she doesn't quit. She's on a mission. We're backing her 100 percent. We'd like to have an answer. We're going to pursue it until we get an answer.

"I've found out that there are a lot of bad people in this town. I hope that one day all of us can eliminate those people. She was my younger sister."

Flynn — who is now the executive director of the state's anti-drug program called "Champions Against Drugs" — comes from a family who was active in sports.

His father, Bobby, attended Dayton on a basketball scholarship and he played in the Brooklyn Dodgers organization for the Hazard, Ky., farm team. While at Hazard in 1951, one of his daddy's teammates included future major league pitcher John Podres, said the younger Flynn. (Podres had a 21-3 mark with an 1.67 earned run average for that season.) The elder Flynn later became a well-known high school basketball referee. Today, Bobby can be seen at UK's home basketball games at Rupp Arena,working for the sports information office and occasionally as a shot clock operator. Now a retired insurance salesman and a former state senator, Bobby serves on Lexington-Fayette Urban County Council.

Doug's mother, Ella Ritchey, was a high school cheerleader, and played basketball and softball. His younger brother, Brad, and sister, Melanie, participated in sports at Bryan Station High School. Brad also works for the sheriff's department in Fayette County.

Doug, who is a Baptist, credits his parents for good

upbringing. "My biggest influences on earth are my mom and dad," he said. "The good Lord has blessed me." His favorite biblical verse is Romans 8:28.

Asked what was his best moment in baseball, Flynn replied, "I better say when I met my wife." He met Olga when he played for the New York Mets as the starting second baseman. In fact, he was introduced to Olga by Pete Rose's would-be second wife, the former Carol Woliung.

"Pete and I were going to a dinner one night and I said, 'Why don't you bring Carol and have her bring somebody to talk to, and we'll talk baseball.' So he did and I married her. She's from Philadelphia and she's a Puerto Rican."

Rose was playing with the Philadelphia Phillies at the time and his future wife, Carol, was a NFL cheerleader for the Philadelphia Eagles as well as the Cincinnati Bengals. "I've heard a lot of people say, 'Is that good news or bad news,' Flynn said of his first meeting with Olga. "But that is good news. We've been married 12 years."

On June 15, 1977, the Reds announced a trade — the famous Tom Seaver deal — involving five players, including Flynn. Cincinnati, seeking to bolster its pitching corps, traded Flynn, pitcher Pat Zachry and two minor league outfielders to New York for pitching star Tom Seaver.

Flynn wasn't too happy about the trade. That meant he would no longer be close to his home in

Lexington where his parents lived. His mom and dad didn't like it, either. "Culture shock, I think, is the word," Flynn said of his parents upon learning about the trade. "And everybody was a little disappointed because of the way the Reds did it."

Dick Wagner, then the executive vice president of the Reds, informed Flynn of the deal. "He just walked in with a piece of paper, saying sign this and you're now the property of the New York Mets. (He didn't say) good luck, no nothing, nothing personal and I'd been there for five years, three in minors and two in major league. You're just a piece of meat. The players were great but this was from the front office and they don't care."

But the trade gave Flynn a chance to be a regular infielder. "After talking to Pete Rose, Johnny Bench and some of the others, they said for me to look at it as a chance to be an everyday ball player," Flynn commented. "(Then-New York manager) Joe Torre was very good for me. He said, 'You're my player, go out and play.' He put me in the lineup my second year and said, 'You are my second baseman.' I played every game in 1978 to '80. It helped me to relax a little bit. New York can be a tough place to play, but they treated me really good." In 1980, Flynn won a Gold Glove Award as a reliable second baseman.

Then, in the spring training of 1981, Flynn became upset when he saw a newspaper headline about his fielding blunders in an exhibition contest. "Only one time did I have a bad relationship (with the media)," he said. "We're playing the Phillies the first game of the spring training. I made two errors. One was a throwing error — I hit a guy in the back — and the other was I missed a ground ball. After the game was over, a writer came up to me and he said, 'Did you not work out?' I said it's the first game, it's spring training. It doesn't count. (But) the New York paper ran a headline, 'Golden boy not so golden.' That really aggravated me." Flynn said the newspaper article, though, was alright, but he didn't appreciate the headline.

On living in the glittering lights of New York City, Flynn said, "It was okay. It was different. I was single and I didn't have a lot of responsibilities. All of your time was playing ball. I lived in Queens for a year and a half, and I lived out on Long Island for two and a half years. It wasn't that bad. Our team stunk. We were bad. The fans treated me good because I played hard and kept my mouth shut. If I made a mistake, I said I made a mistake. Then, of course, I had a country accent and they liked my accent."

Flynn played with the lowly Mets for four and a half seasons before he was sent to the Texas Rangers after the 1981 campaign. But he didn't stay long in the Lone Star state. In August of 1982, the Rangers traded him to Montreal for future considerations.

Later, in 1985, Flynn asked to be released from Montreal. "I wasn't playing," he explained. "It wasn't fun. I went to (general manager) Murray Cook and said I'll just go. I went home to Lexington. I was there about three days." The phone rang and it was Sparky Anderson.

"Do you want to finish the season out here?" asked Anderson, the Detroit Tigers manager.

"Sure," Flynn said.

At Detroit, he played the last two months and hit .255, according to Flynn. "I played one day a week basically for (1984 World Series MVP Alan) Trammell or (Lou) Whitaker," he said. "I went to spring training in 1986, thinking that I was going to be their utility player and all of this (free agent/owner) collusion stuff started happening so I was let go. I was hitting very well — .400 in spring training — and I don't think Sparky Anderson let me go. I think I was let go by Jim Campbell who was the owner of the ballclub. We are trying to see if there was collusion there and I have my agent working on that now.

"I came home and I knew that it was over then. I could have gone back to a couple of minor league clubs and then maybe get back to the big leagues, but I don't know that. It was time to get on with another part of my life."

In all, Flynn played 11 years in the major leagues.

Flynn has met controversial owner Marge Schott of the Cincinnati Reds several times even though she didn't own the team during his playing days at Cincy. Schott officially became the Reds' owner in February of 1985 when major league baseball approved the sale to Schott. But he says they still don't know each other — very well, if any — despite several meetings.

One time in the early 1990s, Schott didn't like his looks, especially his hair, when Flynn came to Cincinnati for an interview for a broadcasting position. The interview had been arranged by baseball Hall of Famer and former teammate Johnny Bench.

"I've met her five times and she doesn't know me," Flynn said of Schott. "I tried to get a job there in broadcasting. We had met because we do the fantasy camps for the Reds. She walked into the room and said, 'Oh honey, your hair is too long to be on TV,' and she walked out of the room. Everybody else approved my interviews. And that was it. So, no, I don't know her and I guess she don't know me."

After retiring from pro baseball, Flynn remained active in sports, playing golf and softball, among others. And, for about 15 months in 1993 and '94, he served as the co-host on "Sports Huddle," a radio sports talk show, with Alan Cutler of Lexington's WLEX-TV (Channel 18).

However, in October of 1994, he quit the daily show in protest because WLAP Radio, which broadcast his show, also carried a controversial program, which contained the foul-mouthed Howard Stern-type language.

Flynn said he wanted to set a good example for the

youngsters. His radio show also didn't accept alcohol advertising because of his position with the state program, Champions Against Drugs.

A few months later, WLAP canceled the "Sports Huddle" show.

7 Dunk Slammer

JAMES LEE

Images of 1978....

President Jimmy Carter flashes his trademark smile.

Pete Rose becomes baseball's highest-paid player.

The Rev. Jim Jones and his cult followers commit mass suicide and execution in Guyana, a small country in South America.

Lt. Gov. Thelma Stovall stirs controversy in Kentucky.

Jane Fonda wins an Oscar for her role in *Coming Home*.

James Lee seals UK's national championship victory over Duke with a game-ending slam dunk.

Nearly two decades have passed and folks still remember Lee's famous "film-highlight" dunk, a speciality he developed when he was 15.

Lee said, "That's a great honor and a great feeling for me. As a kid, I had dreamed of taking the last shot. You play in the back yard a lot of times and you turn around and take that last shot. That was my ultimate dream as a kid and that dream came true for me."

Known as the "King of Dunk," the 6-5, 230-pound Lee had slammed countless of dunks. But his last one at UK — the championship dunk — was the most special of them all. He said he did the slam for the Wildcat fans to show his appreciation for the support they gave him during his four years at Kentucky.

In the early 1970s, when Lee starred at Henry Clay High School in Lexington, he had visions of going to UK. Yes, he thought about playing at Kentucky, even though there weren't many black student-athletes at UK. He didn't have anyone or role models to look up to at the university.

But he decided to do something about that. By signing with the Wildcats, he became a role model for the black youngsters in Lexington, opening the door for their future opportunities. Lee wanted to spread the word about UK.

"Growing up in Lexington, you didn't have the role model that you wanted to see at UK at the time," said Lee, whose dad was a Baptist minister in Lexington. "It was difficult for me to find someone to look up to. (I wanted to show) that we could be part of the institution at UK. That was my purpose (in going to UK) and through that I gained my education and what else could a man ask for? I wanted to give something back to the community and for them to see a black guy succeed.

"It was an opportunity at that time for black athletes. There was a need for making a change and I thought I was a good person to fit that role model."

According to Lee, he and four teammates — Merion Haskins (younger brother of ex-NBA star and current Minnesota Golden Gophers coach Clem Haskins), Larry Johnson, Reggie Warford and Jack Givens — are the first five black graduates at UK from the Wildcat basketball program.

"A lot of people don't realize that," said Lee of the five black players. "They don't have a clue about that. I think that the black athlete who comes through there now needs to know, not that I'm one to get recognized by it. But they need to understand what went on at the time. It was difficult for many other black athletes and students to go through but we stuck it out and I'm very proud of it. I hope the kids see that.

"I have a problem with the NCAA now with all these stipulations and rules (on recruiting). These kids out there now don't know who I am. They don't know the stepping ground. They don't know the history of UK as far as basketball. I think they need to identify. They need to know the Jack Givens, the Reggie Warfords, the Larry Johnsons, the Merion Haskins. I think it is bad (for not knowing about the situation)."

Before deciding on UK, Lee had many scholarship offers. Big-time schools from all over the nation courted him; SEC schools, North Carolina, UCLA, Ohio State.

"There were so many (offers) at one time," Lee said of the recruiting process. "You couldn't keep up with them. It made you want to go out and play a little harder. It was exciting to be accepted around the country as one of the top players."

Besides wanting to be a role model for the black community in Lexington, his family and the school's basketball reputation also influenced him in going to UK, Lee said.

"I knew my father didn't travel as much," he said. "He didn't like airplanes and I wanted him to get to see me play for four more years at home. I thought that was a big plus. I was looking for a school to play and UK had a great basketball tradition."

In 1974, while Lee was being courted by hundreds of schools, the most sought-after high school player in the nation was 6-11 Moses Malone of Petersburg, Va. And Lee got to meet the player in a one-on-one competition in the Derby Classic at Louisville. Guess who won? Lee took the honors.

"It was a good feeling," Lee said of the individual duel with Malone. "I don't know how I beat him. I had never heard of him before. We played in an all-star game and we had had this preliminary (competition). I feel good about that since he became a multi-millionaire."

Malone later made history when he became the first prep basketball player to ink a pro contract. He had decided to skip college. A third-round draft pick in the ABA, the 18-year-old signed a guaranteed four-year pact with the Utah Stars for a total of approximately $600,000.

Some people believed that Kentucky had a "recruiting package deal" when Lee and newly-named Kentucky's "Mr. Basketball" Jack Givens of cross-town Lexington Bryan Station High School signed with the Wildcats in April of 1974.

UK coach Joe B. Hall said there were no package deals, but some critics weren't so sure. Lee, however, sided with Hall, saying the coach was right.

"We made our decision separately but we were happy that we made it (to UK) together," Lee said. "He made up his mind one day and I made up my mind the next day. I think (assistant) coach (Dick) Parsons came back to me and said that Jack is going to sign. I said, 'Well, coach Parsons, give me a day or two.' Then he came back and I said, 'Well, I think I'm ready (to sign).' So UK brought us together. That's how it happened when we announced at the same time."

Before Lee and Givens — both left-handed shooters — came to UK, they were already close friends, even though they competed as rivals in high school. "We knew each other," said Lee who was a 6-6 center at Henry Clay, averaging 25 points and 18 rebounds his senior year. "We were friends. He started out at Henry Clay and then his parents moved out of the Henry Clay district. Then we became competitors. The rivalry was so great that I remember those games real well."

Asked if he beat Givens and Bryan Station most of the time, Lee smiled, "I think we drew up even. It was exciting. Every time we played we had to go to Memorial Coliseum because that was the big game in Lexington. (Fans came) to see us compete against each other. We respected each other enough that we didn't check each other but we knew where the other was."

And the duo later became roommates on road trips their senior year at UK. Today, they still keep in touch. They usually get together in the summer since Givens is busy during the roundball season with his TV broadcasting duties with NBA's Orlando Magic.

During his Wildcat career, Lee didn't start many games. At UK, he was known as the muscular sixth man with a crowd-pleasing, powerful dunk. Had he gone to another college, he would've been a starter. Was he sorry about going to UK?

"Sometimes I think that I have regrets," Lee said. "But overall, in the big picture, I don't have any regrets. I think I would have done it again. The sixth man is now a popular thing at UK and somewhere along the line I feel like I was a part of that (sixth man tradition)."

Lee said he didn't worry about his "sixth man" role on the team. He just wanted to play. Lee, nevertheless, was content as he saw a lot of playing time.

While the 1974-75 Wildcats — led by seniors Kevin Grevey, Jimmy Dan Conner, Mike Flynn and Bob Guyette along with the talented freshmen — had a lot of success and went all the way to the Final Four (where they lost to UCLA), Lee wasn't the happiest person in the world. He was a freshman who even considered transferring.

Lee didn't see a lot of action while his three rookie teammates — Givens, Rick Robey and Mike Phillips — made significant contributions to the squad. During the 1974-75 season, Lee played 148 minutes in 25 games, averaging nearly six minutes.

"It was disturbing," Lee said of his little playing time. "It was kind of difficult to adjust to that. You come out of high school and think you can compete on a college level and you don't see the action. You look up and (realize) you're not playing as much. You scratch your head and wonder what you've done. Dickie Parsons helped me to understand that my time would come and that you just assume you belong to the team."

For Lee, things started to fall in place his sophomore year when Kentucky went to the NIT in New York. He finally saw a lot of playing time. He started 20 games, replacing Robey who injured his knee in mid-season.

Lee finished his second collegiate season with average of 9.3 points and 7.3 rebounds. His high-point total came against a tough Alabama team when he scored 21 points in a 90-85 victory in UK's next-to-last home game at Memorial Coliseum. The win earned UK a post-season bid in the NIT.

In the following season (1976-77), UK found a new home — the massive 24,000-seat Rupp Arena, dubbed by critics as a "white elephant." The Kentucky-Wisconsin season opener on Nov. 27, was the first game ever played in Rupp Arena.

Lee will never forget the opener at the new downtown facility. With ailing 75-year-old Adolph Rupp on hand for the historic occasion, ice-cold Kentucky beat the Badgers 72-64 in a poor-shooting performance which saw the Cats hit 38.2 percent of their shots. Kentucky had problems adjusting to the new hardwood floor in a "home-away-from-home" matchup.

"It was a different experience," said Lee, who scored 11 points in the opener. "It was like moving away from home. It was like visiting. We had problems with practicing (at the new arena). I don't think we practiced but a couple of days before the game. It was like an away game in a sense. That was a big adjustment.

"It (Rupp Arena) was kind of wide open because Memorial Coliseum was closer to the floor. Because we were in a new place, it was a difficult situation, seeing all those people. Being there in front of a crowd, you didn't know how it was going to be. You didn't know what to expect and how the ball was going to bounce even though we practiced. It was a little chill bumping there at times. You got a lump in your stomach. (I wondered if) I'm going to make the first shot."

A couple of weeks later, Kentucky officially dedicated the new arena to Rupp as it whipped Kansas, his alma mater, by a score of 90-63.

As the season progressed, UK sometimes played like a national champion. There were high expectations for the Wildcats, who destroyed opponents, including then second-ranked Notre Dame and Vanderbilt, in several blowouts.

But at College Park, Maryland, UK saw its Final

Four hopes dashed. It dropped to North Carolina and its four-corner offense 79-72 in the NCAA tournament. The day before, the Wildcats took a tour at the White House where they met Vice President Walter Mondale. The 1976-77 Wildcats, nevertheless, finished with an outstanding 26-4 mark, including two NCAA tourney victories over Princeton and VMI. For the season, Lee gunned in an average of nearly 10 points.

As the 1977-78 campaign arrived, Lee and his senior teammates — Givens, Robey and Phillips — had one more chance to win the coveted NCAA championship. They previously had tried three times, but failed each time. Time was running out.

Even though they had already done wonders for the school in winning the NCAA runner-up spot in 1975, winning the NIT championship in 1976 and capturing two SEC titles (1975 and '77), the foursome wanted more. Their goal was to win the NCAA title.

But Kentucky, ranked No. 1 in the pre-season polls, had somewhat of a bumpy start. In the season-opening contest with Southern Methodist University, the Wildcats played without Lee and 6-6 sophomore forward LaVon Williams. The NCAA had suspended them for one game for playing in an organized summer game sponsored by the city of Lexington. The duo watched the game from the bench as UK rolled past the Mustangs behind Givens' game-leading 30 points in a 110-86 victory at Rupp Arena.

Lee said he didn't know about the rule which prohibited players from playing in a non-NCAA sanctioned game.

"I wasn't aware of it," Lee said. "That was just a simple young mistake. I'm from Lexington and they asked me to play (in the summer game). I was trying to do something for the community. That's the way I was looking at it. I don't know why it could be a violation to participate in a game. If you look at the NCAA rules, they got a log book about that thick."

As a Wildcat player, Lee said his best game came in his senior year in UK's 104-81 win over Auburn at Rupp Arena. The 23,000 spectators at the game included three interested scouts from the Boston Celtics — coaches Tom Sanders and K. C. Jones and general manager Red Auerbach. In the victory, Lee pumped in 25 points, which eventually would be his career-high, and grabbed eight rebounds.

Lee later said he didn't know that the Boston officials had attended the game. They sat behind the UK bench. "Somebody told me they were there," he commented. "Evidently they saw something they didn't like because they didn't draft me."

Fourteen games later, Lee and his teammates saw their life-long dream come true. Kentucky won its fifth national title in school history. But the national media wrote that Kentucky players didn't have or weren't allowed to have any fun in their "season without celebration." It was all business in the Wildcat program. Everybody expected the dead-serious Cats to win it all. Anything less than the championship was deemed a failure.

According to Lee, the media's assessment of the Wildcats not having any fun was grossly inaccurate. "A lot of the media said we weren't having any fun, but I thought we had a blast," Lee said. "We had a good time. We were focused on what we had to do, but we had a good time within our surroundings.

"We were there to compete and to win. We weren't there to party. It was senseless of the media to think we were there for anything else. We had fun within our family group of the team. That was all that was necessary. After we won it, we had a blast."

After watching UK's championship victory over Duke in Saint Louis on national television, thousands of UK students came running outside in darkness, celebrating on the streets in or around the campus. They were everywhere. They partied all night, forcing some to skip classes the next day.

Another mass celebration took place in Lexington that victorious night. Approximately 8,000 jubilant fans jammed the airport and loudly cheered the team when it arrived on the scene. It was a very exciting moment that the stunned players, including Lee, will never forget.

"It was a wonderful feeling to come back and see the support that we had," Lee recalled. "It was a surprise. We weren't expecting anybody. We talked on the plane and wondered if anybody would be at the airport. When we came back (home on I-75 the previous week) from Dayton in the Mideast Regional, we saw people on the overpass waving as we were riding on the bus.

"So we were curious what type of reception we would get when we got to the airport. It was unbelievable. It was one of the (most) wonderful welcomes you can get. I felt sorry for the airport officials because they (fans) tore up the airport and things like that. I don't think they minded after what it was all about. It was truly something to see. You get cold chills when you think about those things."

Some say Lee and his mentor, Joe B. Hall, had somewhat of an odd player-coach relationship. They didn't always see eye-to-eye, according to various reports. Lee said that wasn't really the case.

"I think a lot of people didn't understand our relationship," said Lee, one of the so-called 'coolest' players on the squad who rarely displayed emotion. "We had a very unique relationship. A lot of the media thought we didn't get along and that we weren't on the same page. Coach Hall understood me and I understood him. That was the biggest mystery between us. We understood each other, but I don't think anybody else did."

On the floor, the media sitting on the press row across from UK bench would notice that Lee and Hall rarely sat close together on the bench. Some thought they didn't like each other, pointing out that the sixth man traditionally sat next to the head coach. At every opportunity, when Lee sat on the bench, he tried to avoid sitting next to Hall. But he had a legitimate reason.

"If you ever looked at Joe, sitting beside Joe at a game, you would never see the game," explained Lee. "So I had to sit on the end of the bench to get the full sight of the game. And I couldn't sit beside coach Hall because he was hitting me with that (rolled-up) program. I sat on the end of the bench to see what my role would be in the game.

"Nobody asked me so they just assumed that coach Hall and I had our problems. Our relationship was great. He didn't get the respect he deserved at UK after following Rupp. (Following) a legend such as Rupp is tough. It is very difficult to fit in until you get yourself settled and he came in at a tough time, but I respected him for what he did."

During Kentucky's 1977-78 NCAA championship season, Hall didn't coach as much as usual. The players, especially the seniors, knew what their role was and they did the job, Lee explained.

"I don't think coach Hall coached as hard my senior year," he said, "because we told him to relax and we'd win the games — draw up the X's and O's and we'd do the rest. I think after he realized what character we had, he was able to relax. He knew we wanted to win. We didn't want anything short of winning (the title). That's kind of unique."

In the second round of the 1978 NBA draft, Seattle chose Lee, one of four UK seniors selected in the annual draft.

Seattle, at the time, was a rapidly-improving club which had started the season with a dismal 5-17 mark before advancing all the way to the NBA championship series, losing to Washington in seven games. Early in the season, Lenny Wilkens from the front office had taken over the SuperSonics as the head coach and the club found its winning formula en route to the finals.

But Lee didn't make the cut in the training camp and went to Europe.

"They had fallen short of the NBA championship and they kind of had that team molded," Lee said. "They weren't looking for a whole lot, but they looked for a power forward. They kept me as long as they could and two days before the deadline they cut me. There wasn't anywhere else to go to. All of the other teams had their rosters (filled). I went overseas and played in Spain. And I came back and played in a couple of semi-pro leagues. I retired early."

Before retiring, Lee played for the Louisville Catbirds in a growing minor league called the Continental Basketball Association in early 1980s. On the Louisville club, Lee also had a couple of teammates who played at UK — Tom Payne and Dirk Minniefield. Another former UK cager, Dwight Anderson, also performed in the CBA. He played for the Ohio Mixers.

For the past several years, Lee has lived in Louisville where he works for the United Parcel Service (UPS). He drives a package vehicle. He and his wife, Denise, have two children, both girls.

As a former Wildcat star, Lee still keeps track of the Kentucky games, especially on television. He doesn't go to many games in person because his Rupp Arena seats aren't very good.

"My tickets aren't in a great location so I don't go very often," said Lee, who once was upset with the UK program as he and some of the other ex-Wildcats felt like they were not appreciated enough. "I try to go once or twice a year. I like to watch it on TV. I am a TV man now."

Lee certainly wasn't happy to see Kentucky's name being splashed negatively all over the newspapers, radio and television in one of the roundball scandals in the 1980s.

"I read some of the comments from some of the players about getting money," he said. "That disturbed me so I didn't read anything else. I didn't read much about what was going on (later). I tuned myself away from it. I think that (controversy) was trying to disturb the university. If these guys are doing it, then the NCAA needs to look into it and do something about it. I was just disturbed about the players talking about it."

On former UK teammate and ex-Wildcat assistant coach Dwane Casey, who was charged by the NCAA for allegedly putting $1,000 in an express package shipped to a recruit's father, Lee said, "He got one of the rawest deals ever. He is a good man."

Lee acknowledged that UK's basketball program may be overwhelming for some Wildcat players. The demanding pressures of performing successfully and being in the constant spotlight without getting in off-the-court troubles are almost unbearable, especially for the freshmen coming right out of high school.

"It takes a lot to go through the program," he said. "It took a lot of growing up. You just got to be prepared. Kentucky basketball is life to some people and some kids can't handle it. For some players, it is difficult to handle. I think some of the older players (ex-Wildcats) can help but NCAA rules won't let us (get involved).

"There was a lot of pressure to win at UK, but that was what we tried to do. If the kids give 110 percent, you can't fault them. There's a lot of pressure on these kids. The fans demand a lot. They demand that you win. They don't want you to lose one game."

After the 1995 New Year's Day interview for this book ended at his new home in Louisville, Lee commented that he looked forward to watching the Kentucky-Louisville game on CBS television network later in the afternoon. But when he was at UK, Lee wished he had the opportunity to face star Darrell Griffith and the Cards.

"I would have loved to play them back then," Lee said. "They had a lot of talent. It would have been a dream game. It would have been very competitive. But I didn't care who we played back then." Needless to say, Lee was five years too late as UK and Louisville finally met in a post-season tournament matchup in 1983.

By the way, in that New Year's Day contest, fifth-ranked Kentucky lost to U of L by two points, an 88-86 verdict, before 19,841 fans at Freedom Hall.

After the buzzer sounded, you can bet that Lee certainly wasn't a real happy man. UK's loss to Louisville probably meant that he would get a little aggravation at work. The Cardinal fans at UPS would be all over him, teasing or bragging about how great Louisville was.

"Wait 'till next year," Lee would tell them, adding that UK still holds a commanding lead in the series with rival U of L.

8 Knoxville Kid
CHRIS GETTELFINGER

Chris Gettelfinger — a former 6-2 guard who played on Kentucky's last national championship team as a walk-on freshman in 1978 — is one of the approximately 18,000 fans who witnessed what is arguably the greatest NCAA tournament game ever when Duke edged Kentucky 104-103 in overtime in 1992.

"I drove up to Philadelphia and went to the Kentucky-Duke game when Christian Laettner hit that last shot," said Gettelfinger, who lives in Knoxville, Tenn. "That was the most disappointing game I ever witnessed in my life. When they lost to Duke, I actually felt worse about that game than any game I'd ever been involved in."

When Kentucky is playing in a post-season tournament, you can bet Gettelfinger and his wife, Jill, will be there.

In 1995, they attended the Kentucky-North Carolina matchup in the NCAA Southeast Regional finals in Birmingham, Ala. They came home very disappointed as the poor-shooting Cats lost 74-61.

"I've been to every tournament game that they've been in during the last three or four years," said Gettelfinger. "My wife didn't go (to the Kentucky-Duke contest), but she has been everywhere else. She was in

Charlotte when we played Wake Forest and Florida State (in 1993). We went to New Orleans for the Michigan game (in 1993 Final Four). We also go up (to Lexington) and go to some of the games during the year."

Despite getting her degree from University of Tennessee, Jill loves the Wildcats, said her husband, showing a picture of her dressed in a Wildcat blue outfit.

"She's the biggest Kentucky fan in Knoxville," said Gettelfinger, who married her in 1992. "I guarantee you that. My wife's a pretty good looker. When we went to the Michigan game, she wore her blue outfit and she was all painted up with glitter in her hair and UK blue stuff hanging on her. She was getting a lot of attention at the games."

And the Gettelfingers make sure they don't have anything planned on the night Kentucky invades Tennessee in Knoxville. Their home, located near the Tennessee River, is only several minutes away from the 24,535-seat Thompson-Boling Arena. They go to every UK-at-UT game, said the former Wildcat player.

"I've seen Kentucky play more in Knoxville than I have seen Tennessee play," he said, "and that's the truth. I've probably been to 10 Kentucky games in the last seven or eight years here in Knoxville and probably only been to seven UT games. I don't watch Tennessee basketball that much."

Gettelfinger also pointed out that he was especially glad when the nation's top hoops prospect in 1994-95, Ron Mercer, picked Kentucky over Tennessee in a tough recruiting battle. A native of Nashville, Tenn., the 6-7 Mercer averaged 26.3 points and nearly seven rebounds in guiding Oak Hill Academy (in Mouth of Wilson, Va.) to a 31-3 mark during the 1994-95 campaign.

However, don't get the impression that Gettelfinger doesn't like UT at all. He admits that he is a big follower of the Vols football program. So is Jill. They have season tickets to UT football games. And Gettelfinger offers an opinion about the Vols rising quarterback star.

"Peyton Manning is going to be a tough quarterback in the next few years," he said.

Before he came to UK in 1977, Gettelfinger played basketball at Knoxville Catholic High School where he earned All-American and All-State honors. An excellent shooter and ball-handler, Gettelfinger averaged 25 points a game for three years from his sophomore to senior year.

But during his senior year, he suffered an illness which forced him to miss significant portions of the basketball season. He got mononucleosis, an infectious disease which usually affects young adults in their late teens and early 20s.

That cost the red-haired Gettelfinger many scholarship offers from major universities. And he was unhappy with the remaining offers he had, mostly from the smaller colleges. So he decided to walk on at Kentucky. He wanted to be a part of the school's strong roundball program. He had been interested in the Wildcats since he attended coach Joe B. Hall's summer basketball camp at UK while in high school. In addition, UK was not far from his home. Lexington is only a three-hour drive from Knoxville.

Gettelfinger said he didn't have any regrets about walking on at UK, whereas he could have received a scholarship and become a star at other places. He might have gone to UT had it offered him a scholarship. When he was ready to go college, he was certainly concerned about leaving his Knoxville home and the family. He wasn't sure of himself. He was a typical college-bound young man.

"When I first went to UK, I had apprehensions about leaving Knoxville," Gettelfinger commented. "In the beginning when you left, it was scary. There's lots of reasons (for that). It's scary to do interviews when you're young. It's scary to be set on a pedestal and be afraid you're going to fall off. It's scary to play on TV. It's scary to play in front of people.

"I was homesick. You leave (home) and you don't

know what's out there. Everybody gets homesick. Anybody who tells you they're not doesn't have a heart. I knew that there was enough out there to push me over the edge to go. But when you leave, you leave everybody behind."

During his freshman year, Gettelfinger became good friends with sophomore Tim Stephens, a Wildcat guard from McCreary County near the Kentucky-Tennessee border in the south central part of the state. They ran around together a lot. That made Gettelfinger's adjustment to college life a lot easier.

"He was a year ahead of me and had just gone through it," Gettelfinger said of Stephens.

Stephens, however, didn't finish his career at Kentucky. In the early part of the 1978-79 campaign, the 6-3 junior decided to transfer to Cumberland College. He was frustrated with his lack of playing time and felt like he did not get a fair chance to play.

While at McCreary County (now McCreary Central) High, Stephens led the state in scoring with an average of 36 points a contest his senior year. He was so talented that Hall once compared Stephens with ex-NBA superstar Jerry West of the Los Angeles Lakers.

So Gettelfinger really missed Stephens when his friend left the UK campus shortly after the Christmas holidays. That meant he would have to practice or play without Stephens around in the spring semester.

Assistant coach Dick Parsons was another individual who helped Gettelfinger. "He tried to make a positive influence and he did it for a lot of people," said Gettelfinger. "He stayed positive and focused. He didn't get all bogged down when everything went wrong. Dick Parsons was the glue and butter of the team that won the (national) championship.

"From Joe B. Hall's perspective, he had a lot of different pressures that Dick didn't have, like dealing with the alumni, expectations and financial pressures.... Kentucky basketball is a big business. Dick was on just one level right underneath that. Dick is a very smart man and he chose to disassociate himself 100 percent from the problems that Joe had. He understood the psychology and transformations of people and what made them work."

Gettelfinger agrees that Kentucky's 1977-78 campaign was a "season without celebration." The national press had criticized Hall's "business-like" approach in coaching, arguing the Wildcats took the game too seriously and had no fun. Basketball is only a game — not life or death, they wrote.

The Wildcats had capped their remarkable 30-2 season with a national title victory over Duke 94-88 in Saint Louis as red-hot Jack "Goose" Givens poured in a classic 41 points. Even though Gettelfinger saw minimal action in only nine games, playing 12 minutes and scoring a total of two points, the so-called "fun-less" season turned out be a very valuable lesson for him. It would help him later on in life, explained Gettelfinger, now a well-to-do businessman who holds interest in many properties in the Knoxville area.

"It was a season without celebration — absolutely 100 percent," he said. "You can laugh at it now because we won it. That's what made it worthwhile. And I thank God for that because if we hadn't won, I may have looked at everything a little bit differently. (Winning) shouldn't make or break a life or a lifestyle, but it does create a lot of positives. I have no fear of failure anymore in life whatsoever. This started out by being on that team. In business, I think I would be just as satisfied now to settle down and retire young if I had any failures. I don't have any pressure to absolutely succeed.

"But that year, I think that the pressure was on everybody. It was not just one-sided pressure. The pressure didn't come from one place. The pressure came from the four seniors, too. They knew it was their last chance.

There were lots of expectations. There was pressure on the coaching staff. They knew that they had built the nucleus of a team. They had been to the UCLA game (in the 1975 Final Four). They had been to the NIT finals. They knew what their opportunities were.

"The alumni were putting pressure on. The fans were putting pressure on. Everybody wanted to be successful. Everybody had the pressure. When we won it, everybody felt relieved and was very happy. Everybody was under the gun. The fans felt like we had made it back into UK tradition. When we won that championship game (against Duke), it was like, 'Okay, we did it. Now we can have more fun.' "

With his ecstatic teammates cheering on from the bench, Gettelfinger, playing in a reserve role, once scored six points in less than a minute remaining when UK, led by Kyle Macy's 20 points, whipped Mississippi State 89-67 at Starkville. The hustling junior hit all three of his field goals in that 1980 game. The six points, as it turned out, would be the most he ever scored in one game at UK.

His teammates teased him about scoring a lot of points in such a short period of time, saying he could've gotten 100 points had he played the whole game. "That (game) always kind of stuck in my mind," he said. "I always remembered it."

When playing at home, Gettelfinger — who was awarded a scholarship by Hall after his sophomore year — was the guy whom UK students loved to cheer on when he entered the matchup. He was a crowd favorite. They always yelled "shoot, shoot," every time the little-used guard had the ball, even if he was 50 feet away from the basket.

His last home game at Rupp Arena was a special one. The Senior Day. Gettelfinger and 6-8 forward Freddie Cowan were the only seniors on the 1980-81 Wildcat squad. And Kentucky was playing host to then-No. 2 LSU, which was attempting to become the first conference team to go unbeaten in 25 years.

In a customary pre-game ceremony honoring the seniors, a then-record Rupp Arena crowd of 24,011 sang "My Old Kentucky Home" with ex-Gov. Happy Chandler leading the way. It was an emotional time for these two players and their families.

"That's the one thing I remember," said Gettelfinger, who received his business administration degree in four years. "I didn't cry outwardly, but I think inside I understood emotionally. (Senior Day) is like a badge of the film that is to the person individually and they do a very good job of specializing with the seniors.

"Senior Day is for the parents, too. When they bring the parents out on the floor, that's the one time the parents get to feel the school's tradition. They're playing 'My Old Kentucky Home' and stuff. You can actually feel the tradition. I know that my mom and dad and others had finally gotten a little bit of the taste of what it's like to walk out in front of all those people." (His mother today lives near her son's home, while his dad died several years ago. Gettelfinger also has two brothers and one sister.)

Gettelfinger said that Chandler "wasn't the greatest singer, but boy, he sang it with a lot of enthusiasm. He was an interesting man. With all he did in his life — baseball commissioner, governor, whatever he did in his life — he had it down. He wasn't a good singer, but he understood. He went out there and he was the Kentucky person singing 'My Old Kentucky Home.' That's what it meant to him that we're Kentuckians. I really enjoyed the way he sang it."

For the record, emotional Kentucky used its balanced scoring attack to defeat a strong LSU team 73-71. Four Wildcats — Sam Bowie, Dirk Minniefield, Chuck Verderber and Melvin Turpin — had 11 points each and Cowan added 10 points in the victory. Gettelfinger did not see action.

LSU, led by 6-7 All-American forward Durand Macklin, later went to the NCAA Final Four at a time when the nation expressed grief over the assassination attempt on President Reagan's life. The Tigers finished the year with a 31-5 record, including 17-1 in the SEC. Kentucky, meanwhile, went 22-6 for the year after losing to Alabama-Birmingham in the NCAA tourney.

On the stunning loss to UAB, Gettelfinger said, "It was a big fat disappointment. We had a great team that year and we weren't supposed to get beat by them. The only way to go for the coaching staff, players and everybody was to just go their separate ways for a few days. That's basically what happened (afterwards).

"There were only two seniors, me and Freddie, in that game. One thing Joe B. (Hall) understands is that after that's over, when his player finishes, he was their friend. He would be there to listen or be there to help."

During his junior year, while working on his business degree, Gettelfinger once signed up for an interesting course that he didn't need. It was "a side course," as he calls it, or an elective. Instead of taking an easy subject, he took a course which focused on animal pathology.

"I chose animal pathology as a filler course instead of just taking it easy," he said. "I wanted to take some learning. That was the most interesting (subject) and actually the hardest. We actually got into dissecting horses and the whole structure of horses and the intestines, the whole deal. That was hard. I liked it a lot, though.

"I have a farm now. I have horses, cattle and stuff. We always had a farm (when I was) growing up. I use it (from that class) today in caring for all of my horses and cattle. I could actually see how people would want to be veterinarians. We studied the horse, basically anatomy stuff as much as doctors who get into the humans."

Asked what grade he got for that class, Gettelfinger replied, "I got a B."

Gettelfinger does not believe UK's basketball program is overexposed. The players enjoy the adulation that comes with the program and the fans like to read or talk about the Wildcats, he explained.

"One reason is that when you're young and inside the program, there can never be too much exposure," Gettelfinger commented. "That's what you live for.

"Two, I know why sports are successful now. Sports are an escape for everybody that's out there working hard for a living — beating it, fighting it, fighting economics, taxes, pressure. It's an escape. They need things to talk about other than their problems and their pressures in life. And that's what sports allow. People have conversations. It's positive. Even when you're talking about a negative — such and such got kicked off, such and such got hurt — it's a positive. A psychologist could tell you it's a positive. What people are doing is bending their frustrations or releasing things.

"So I can't see, as long as people want to talk about it, I can't see how it's too much (exposure). If it is too much, then you'll walk away from it. But people writing, talking and buying newspapers, they enjoy it. I get *The Cats' Pause* (magazine). I enjoy looking through it — forty minutes to an hour — thinking about somebody else's problems besides myself. What's UK's strategy for basketball? Who they are going to recruit? I'm not directly involved anymore and so I look at their problems. It's like a release for me. I view it and think about it, but I don't take them home to bed with me."

Gettelfinger has an interesting theory about UK's strong basketball tradition. Although winning is a contributing factor, Kentucky basketball has developed into one of the nation's most tradition-rich programs because of its locale, he said.

"When you ride the downs in a big city, you just change teams to whoever is on top," he explained. "When you ride the downs in Lexington and Knoxville, there's nowhere else to go to. So you ride (with) the team. That's probably what makes tradition because the fans don't have anywhere else to go. You feel bad at lows and you feel (great) at highs. You go back and forth and it takes a long period of time.

"I don't believe that if you were in a major, major city that you would have the traditions like Tennessee football and Kentucky basketball. I don't believe it would work in other places. You probably couldn't take Kentucky basketball and move it to New York. It wouldn't work."

Cawood Ledford — who was popularly known the Voice of the Wildcats — retired in 1992 after a long illustrious career in broadcasting. Ironically, his last game as a Wildcat announcer was the classic Kentucky-Duke game in the NCAA tournament.

Like many UK fans, Gettelfinger misses Cawood. Before coming to UK, he even listened to the legendary announcer on the 50,000-watt WHAS Radio from his Knoxville home. "He was like my tie to the past," he said. "He was tradition. He was my familiarity. I even heard Cawood down here (in Tennessee) when I was little."

Unlike most young adults in their twenties or younger, Gettelfinger said the older generation sorely misses Cawood's journalistic colorful voice.

"The older people — 35, 40 and above — are the ones who are having a hard time in missing him, but all good things come to an end," he said. "I'm kind of glad to see for Cawood that he left pretty much on time. He left with some health and that he didn't actually just push it out to where he started. You know, in another 10 or 12 years, he could have started to lose maybe his perspective and not be as good.

"Wasn't the last game the Duke-Kentucky game that he called? He called the greatest game. That's amazing. That was the best college game that I have ever seen. So maybe it was destiny that he was set to go after that game."

9 From Harlan to Lexington

DICK PARSONS

When Joe B. Hall retired from his head coaching post at UK in 1985, Dick Parsons was one of several names mentioned as a possible replacement.

But he didn't get the job. Eddie Sutton, then the head coach at Arkansas, was the one UK chose to be its new head basketball coach.

Parsons — who had previously quit his job as assistant coach at Kentucky in the spring of 1980 after many years at the helm — said he wasn't disappointed when Kentucky hired the Razorback mentor.

"I'm not sure that I was the right person for the job," Parsons explained. "I was interviewed for it, but I didn't make an official application. A lot of former players and other UK fans encouraged me to ask for an interview. So I did that.

"If you want someone with a Kentucky background, with my qualifications, I was willing to do it. But that was a decision that the (search) committee would have to make. And they chose to go outside the Kentucky scheme of things, which was fine. At the time, they wanted someone who had head coaching experience. That's when we hired Eddie Sutton. Sutton is a very fine basketball coach."

It wasn't the only opportunity Parsons had to be the head coach. Earlier, many schools, including several SEC institutions, wanted him to come for an interview. He politely said no. He wasn't interested.

"I didn't want to leave Kentucky," Parsons said. "I had chances to become the head coach at very fine schools, but I never pursued them. I was content with my role at UK. My family was happy in Lexington. I knew every day I was outside the boundaries of the state of Kentucky, I'd be homesick."

Said former UK player Chris Gettelfinger, "He got out of coaching still fairly young. He could have been a (head) coach anyplace he wanted to be. He could have gone on in that direction if he wanted to. But I think he actually chose to stay away from that absolute chaos (that come with the head coaching job)."

Four years later, Parsons played a part in UK's search for a new coach. In March of 1989, then-UK president Dr. David Roselle appointed him to an eight-person search committee to screen coaching candidates after Sutton resigned in the midst of NCAA investigation of the school's roundball program. During the nightmarish campaign of 1988-89, Sutton guided the Wildcats to their first losing season (13-19) in 62 years.

Joining Parsons on the committee were Dr. Charles Wethington Jr, now the UK president who was the chancellor of the UK Community College System; ex-Wildcat roundball players William Sturgill, Bobby Watson and Terry Mobley; retired prep basketball coach S. T. Roach; and UK faculty members Robert Lawson and Peggy Meszaros.

Parsons was somewhat surprised, but delighted that UK was able to lure Rick Pitino away from his hometown of New York City, the media capital. Athletic director C. M. Newton was largely responsible for bringing Pitino to Lexington, Parsons said.

"I credit coach Newton with Pitino being at UK," Parsons said. "I thought he went the extra mile to persuade him that we needed him... that he was the right person for the task. If he was looking for utopia as it related to basketball, he'd find it at UK and I think he has."

What if the charismatic Pitino hadn't agree to come to Kentucky? Would Parsons be interested in coaching again? No, according to Parsons, who was working as the director of planned giving for UK's development office, a position he still holds. He had someone else in mind to be the head coach at Kentucky if Pitino didn't come.

"Had it developed just that way, my recommendation would have been that coach Newton would have taken the squad," Parsons said. "I think maybe he was willing to do that if we were unable to hire the person we wanted."

When the NCAA penalized UK for rules violations in May of 1989, Parsons thought its tough sanctions weren't fair. Especially when comparing to other schools which had been placed on probation for various infractions. Kentucky was placed on a three-year probation, including two years of no post-season tournaments, scholarship limitations, among others.

Parsons said, "The university administration made some pretty strong decisions and I thought they did some things to show good faith and the NCAA fired both barrels at us. I don't think we merited that kind of punishment. I think Dr. Roselle made changes and decisions in good faith, thinking that it would impress the NCAA. But I think the NCAA totally disregarded the moves that Dr. Roselle so directed."

In recent years, the NCAA has made efforts to revise the rules. But Parsons believes the organization can do more by simplifying the rules.

"The rules are very complex," Parsons pointed out. "There's has been a lot of changes down through the years. But there could be more improvement in the rules. I don't see an effort being made to do that (in simplification of the rules).

"I think it's important to stress what the rules are — try to teach your players and the coaches what the rules are and what you have to avoid. I don't think any coach wants to go through that turmoil of having NCAA problems."

During his college days at UK, Parsons never had the opportunity to participate in the NCAA Final Four. He was a freshman when the Fiddlin' Five squad won the national championship in 1958. He wasn't on the varsity team, but he was a key contributor to the program.

"We knew them all quite well," Parsons said of the Fiddlin' Five, "because the freshman team (16-1) was a fairly large squad and we practiced against the varsity. We competed against them throughout the year. In fact, in a scrimmage or so, we were able to defeat them but that, of course, was unusual. That was when they would "fiddle around" and not play very well.

"So coach Rupp gave that squad the name, 'The Fiddlin' Five,' because they just did not seem interested and didn't play as well on some occasions. But when they wanted to play, they were really tough and did an outstanding job. It was a real thrill to go in as a freshman and see a team strive and jell at just the right time and win the NCAA."

However, Parsons did go to the Final Four a couple of times as an assistant at UK under coach Joe B. Hall.

His first trip came in 1975 when All-American Kevin Grevey and the Wildcats advanced all the way to the finals before losing to UCLA in mentor John Wooden's last game as the coach. Although the season ended on a disappointing note, Kentucky, nevertheless, finished with a 26-5 worksheet, including a stunning 92-90 upset of unbeaten and top-ranked Indiana in the Mideast Regional finals. It was one of Kentucky's more memorable seasons.

And Parsons remembers a late February incident during that season involving Grevey in Tuscaloosa, Ala. It happened on the day before No. 7 Kentucky and No. 5 Alabama were to meet for the SEC championship.

At the motel, where the team stayed, Grevey had missed the team bus which took the players and coaches to the gym for an afternoon practice. When the squad began its shooting practice, Grevey somehow showed up. He had taken a cab.

Grevey certainly got his money's worth for that quick ride as he barely made the practice. While he rode, Grevey had engaged in a "small talk" conversation with the taxi driver.

"Who are you?" asked the driver.

"I'm a Kentucky basketball player."

"You mean to tell me that the bus left you, the coaching staff left you!"

"Oh, yes, they just left me there."

"You must not be that good."

The cab driver apparently didn't follow basketball very closely as Grevey was a big-time star who eventually finished his collegiate career as the school's all-time second-leading scorer with 1,801 points. (Since then, Grevey has dropped to No. 5 on the career scoring list.)

And, at that practice, not one word was mentioned

about the team leaving him at the motel, according to Parsons.

After the practice, Parsons confronted Grevey.

"Where were you?"

"I decided to lay down for a few moments and fell asleep," Grevey replied.

"How did you get down here?" Parsons asked.

"Well, there was a taxi cab driver and I told him to get to the coliseum as fast as he could."

The next day saw the Cats — who had played most of the first half without Grevey — rally to win the regionally-televised contest 84-79 over the Crimson Tide after being down 12 points in the second half. Grevey, however, was the one who saved the game for Kentucky, finishing with 16 points on 7-of-11 field goal shooting.

Kentucky had struggled in the early going. An angry Hall complained that Grevey wasn't doing anything in the first eight minutes of the contest and the bespectacled coach sent the player to the sidelines. After getting blasted by Hall, Parsons and assistant Lynn Nance at the halftime, Grevey returned early in the second half and sparked the Cats to a key victory before a sellout crowd of over 15,000.

A couple of weeks later, both Kentucky and Alabama ended up in a tie for the SEC title with a 15-3 league mark. Like Kentucky, the Crimson Tide, coached by ex-Wildcat player C. M. Newton, participated in the NCAA tournament where they lost to Arizona State 97-94 in the first round of the West Regional. It was Alabama's first-ever appearance in the NCAA tournament.

On his second journey to the Final Four, Parsons had more fun. Kentucky (30-2) won the 1978 NCAA title. He doesn't agree with the critics who called UK's 1977-78 campaign a season without celebration because of undue pressure placed on the squad.

"There was always the comment that the Kentucky team wasn't having any fun," Parsons recalled. "But I can assure you that we had an awful lot of fun throughout that year. We lost a couple of games to Alabama and LSU (both road matchups). When it was all over with, it's a real thrill to have been part of that team and win the NCAA title. It's something that I think about real often today.

"Competition even in those days was very tough, but everyone in the country thought Kentucky had the best players and should win it. We had a very mature team, serious-minded team. We could play a game at a fast pace or at a slow pace. We were a very unselfish team. The team shot 54 percent throughout the year. They could play under pressure. We defeated some real good teams along the way. Of course, the game against Duke in the finals was a very difficult game. We had it under control pretty much. They (Blue Devils) made a little run at the end of the game, but we were able to pull it out."

Besides the NCAA, there is another post-season tournament that Parsons will never forget.

The season after Kentucky had dropped to UCLA in the NCAA title game, the young Wildcats saw themselves wrestling with an uncharacteristic 10-10 mark in mid-February in 1976. Although UK had lost several key seniors — Grevey, Jimmy Dan Conner, Mike Flynn and Bob Guyette — from the previous season, everyone was asking, "What's wrong with Kentucky?"

Kentucky, however, bounced back to win the remaining six games in the regular season to earn a post-season tournament bid. No, the Cats — who had promising sophomores Jack Givens, James Lee, Mike Phillips and Rick Robey along with junior Larry Johnson and senior Reggie Warford — weren't good enough for the NCAA because of their 16-10 mark. The NIT, however, was interested and invited them to its annual party in New York. The Cats accepted, making their first trip to the Big Apple since the days of the gambling scandal in the early 1950s.

And the surprising Wildcats salvaged a near-disastrous season by winning the NIT in one of the school's most incredible seasons ever. To capture the tournament, UK had to defeat four opponents — Niagara, Kansas State, Providence and North Carolina-Charlotte (coached by ex-Transy mentor Lee Rose).

"The most interesting experience was winning the NIT title in 1976," Parsons said. "At the time, we were 10-10 during the season and we started winning. We won all of our remaining SEC games. We went to New York. We didn't even bring enough clothes. We thought we'll just go up and maybe win a game or two and be back home. But we ended up being in New York for 10 days.

"It was like playing in a state tournament, winning game after game, developing a lot of friends along the way and crowd support. That (NIT crown) was probably one of our greatest accomplishments. I almost equate that with winning the NCAA title. It was one of the most fun times in tournament's play. Much more fun than the participation in the NCAA."

The famous Bobby Knight slap.

As most Wildcat fans would remember, Joe B. Hall and his Wildcats were getting blown out in an early December game of 1974 by a strong Indiana squad in Bloomington. Coach Bobby Knight featured stars Scott May and Kent Benson on his Hoosiers squad.

In the famous second-half episode, Knight and Hall engaged in a heated discussion on the floor as the Indiana mentor complained of an official's call against his team. And in a few moments, Knight slapped Hall across the back of the head, ending their conversation.

Parsons, who was on the bench as an assistant, didn't see the slap but said, "I've seen coach Knight do that on many occasions, however I don't think it was done with any ill intent. But I think it would've better had he not touched coach Hall."

Kentucky lost the game 98-74. Some said the loss was the season's turning point for the Wildcats, who were coming off a disappointing 13-13 season in 1973-74. Even though the campaign had just begun, some had already given up on UK.

"That game probably taught us more about how to play that particular year than any one game ever since I had been at UK," Parsons said. "We were about 20 some points behind and there was a charge call — an Indiana player charged against Jerry Hale. Coach Knight jumped up and complained about it. The game was almost over. Coach Hall wondered why would Bobby Knight be up complaining. Then that (slap) incident took place. (Later in the NCAA tourney), we defeated them in Dayton. And all of that lead up to the fact that in the end we won the game which was important.   So the slap was well worth it because we did everything that happened in that particular game to inspire our team to defeat them in Dayton."

Asked if Hall and Knight were ever close, Parsons said, "I don't know. I can't answer that question."

The Big Orange.
The House of Horrors.
The Tennessee Vols.
Stokely Athletics Center.
Ray Mears.
Knoxville.

In the eyes of UK fans, those were ugly, dreaded words that they had to face every year.

The toughest place to play as a Kentucky assistant? "It had to be Tennessee," Parsons said. "I remember one year I told coach Hall there was no way I'd scout Tennessee. I told him there was no way they could keep us from scoring. And they didn't keep us from scoring. (In 1975) we scored 100 points (actually 98) in the game but they scored 103.

"It was just frustrating because we didn't always play well in Knoxville. Tennessee pointed for that particular game (with Kentucky). They'd lose the game leading up to the Kentucky game and they would lose a game or so afterwards. The press would treat the game in such manner that they would get the Tennessee team all fired up.

"I can always recall Marvin West, a sportswriter for the *Knoxville News-Sentinel*, would come up and see us play the game prior to our playing Tennessee. He would get some quotes for the paper which would give the Tennessee players a little more incentive. We subscribed to the paper. I remember one time and it was a day or so before the Tennessee game that (Rick) Robey was quoted as saying we would definitely defeat Tennessee. Well, he didn't say it quite that way but that's what was spreading.

"Tennessee always did such a great job, and continued to do so down the through the years. It was a very difficult place to play. Certainly, they have the upper hand on Kentucky. Thinking back to the last 20 or 30 years, Tennessee won a lot of the games in Knoxville."

While the head coach of the Vols from 1962 to '77, Mears posted an even 15-15 mark against Kentucky with a majority of his victories taking place before the friendly crowds in Knoxville. Mears was 8-12 against Adolph Rupp and 7-3 versus Hall.

When he coached at UK, Parsons didn't like to spend a lot of time recruiting high school kids. But that was a part of his job description.

"I don't think any coach will tell you that they enjoy recruiting," Parsons said. "The recruiting part of college coaching is the most difficult part. That's the part where you tend to get yourself into some trouble if you're not careful. The rules are very complex. The interpretation of the rules are not the same. You are (trying) to interpret those rules the way the NCAA officials see them. There was a lot of confusion about the rules."

By the way, he had a couple of recruiting stories in mind. One involved Kevin Grevey, a prep superstar from Taft High School in Hamilton, Ohio, who was being recruited by UK in 1971. A local university was recruiting the player vigorously and that school was Miami of Ohio. Other Ohio schools — Cincinnati and Ohio State — also pursued Grevey. He was under tremendous pressure to sign with a hometown university.

After Grevey told UK coaches that he was coming to Kentucky, he began to have second thoughts. Parsons suspected the other schools had persuaded him on the fact that he couldn't play at UK.

"He called and said he wouldn't be coming to UK," Parsons said. "So we convinced him to come for a second visit (to Lexington). We hid him out for a couple of days and we had to recruit him for the second time. I think coaches from Miami came down and tried to find him. But they were not going to find him. There was no way. What we did wasn't illegal. It was perfectly legal to have a second visit at that time. We didn't violate any rules. But it was interesting to note that he felt that he couldn't play at UK and he went on to be one of the biggest players we ever had." (After UK, Grevey also played in the NBA for 10 years. He is currently serving as a radio sports announcer in Washington, D.C.)

Another recruiting episode. On June 1, 1979, Ralph Sampson, the highly-recruited 7-4 prepster from Harrisonburg, Va., held a massive press conference to announce his college choice. Most basketball observers assumed he would sign with Kentucky.

"We had a telephone hookup with him," Parsons said of Sampson. "He told us he was coming to UK and signing with us the next day. We had a Lear jet waiting at the airport. Coach Hall was doing his radio show and I was with him. I was going to complete the radio show and he (Hall) was going on to get on the Lear jet to fly to get Sampson.

"We were listening to the announcement and at the last minute Sampson hesitated a bit. We thought he was going to say Kentucky, but then he decided he was going to Virginia."

Another highly-regarded high school star by the name of Sam Bowie, who had signed with Kentucky, was stunned with Sampson's announcement.

"When I was playing in the all-star games coming out of high school, Ralph and I had talked about both of us going to UK," Bowie said in an interview in 1990. "He said that he was definitely going to UK and it was going to be exciting for me to be playing alongside of a guy like Ralph Sampson.

"But, at the last moment, (because of) some pressure from his mother to stay in the state, he decided to sign with Virginia. A lot of people really don't realize how close it was for the two of us to be playing at UK. Those would have been exciting years with Ralph. I was under the assumption that he was coming to UK. When I heard that he signed with the University of Virginia, I was shocked."

In the spring of 1980, Parsons decided to quit coaching when the NCAA reduced the coaching staff from four to three persons. He could've stayed on at UK and become a full-time recruiter. But Parsons said no.

"I knew that I would not enjoy being a full-time recruiter," Parsons recalled. "You'd really be removed from the coaching aspect of the game. That's when I decided that I would do something else."

With Parsons' retirement, Leonard Hamilton, now the head coach at Miami (Florida), became Hall's No. 1 assistant. Hamilton got a new title for his position in October of 1980 in becoming UK's first associate basketball coach.

When the SEC tournament was revived in 1979 after a 26-year absence, Joe B. Hall and his coaching staff were one of the most vocal opponents of the conference tourney.

"We did not like the SEC tournament," Parsons said. "It was exciting to the fans. They play it strictly for financial reasons, in my opinion. I think it will really hurt your chances later in the NCAA play. It drains off a lot of energy at a critical time in the year when the teams are already tired and physically worn out."

Before retiring, Hall's coaching record in the SEC tournament was 10-6 in seven appearances, including one title in 1984.

Before coming to UK in 1957 from Harlan County in the mountains, Parsons was a four-sports star and an outstanding student at Harlan High School. It is the same school where UK Fabulous Five member Wallace Jones graduated from several years earlier.

Growing up in a small coal mining community called Yancey, Parsons — who was born at home — came from a large family. His father, a former school teacher, was a bookkeeper for a coal mining company. His mother was a devoted housewife, busy raising nine children.

"There's not a lot to do (in Yancey) except get together with all the youngsters in the neighborhood and we'd play baseball, basketball, football or whatever sport was in season," Parsons said of his childhood. "I would say that, on an organized level, I probably started playing basketball on our grade school team when I was in the fifth grade. Later on when I was in the seventh and eighth grade, we would compete against some of the surrounding schools and we would play on outdoor courts.

"But in Yancey we had a gymnasium and we could play there. We would hook up two wires to turn the lights on so we could play there at night. That's what we spent all of our time doing. Every free moment was spent playing. That was pretty much the beginning of my career as a player."

Back then most people didn't have television sets in their homes. Television, a new technology development, was considered a luxury item at the time. So, instead of watching the Cats on TV like most people do today, Parsons had to listen to the games on the radio. By the time he arrived on the UK campus, the Kentucky games had been televised only three times with the first-ever TV game taking place in 1951.

The Fabulous Five group of 1947-48 was probably the first Kentucky team he followed, Parsons said. "I would have been about 9 or 10 at the time," he recalled. "I would pretend to be Ralph Beard, Wallace Jones and other players. I think every Kentucky youngster wants to grow up being a Wildcat and I was no different than youngsters all over the state of Kentucky. It made a great impression on me to be able to listen on the radio and learn about Ralph Beard, Wallace Jones, (Cliff) Barker and Kenny Rollins and all other players. It was quite exciting."

However, Parsons almost didn't go to UK. He had planned to attend a college in Georgia after completing high school. He had family connections at Georgia Southern where two of his brothers had previously attended.

But his high school basketball coach Joe Gilly wanted Parsons to reconsider. The coach thought Parsons could make it successfully at Kentucky.

"I guess I was thinking of playing baseball more so than basketball," Parsons said. "I had pretty much decided that's where I would go. Kentucky had offered me a scholarship through coach Joe Gilly and I thought a lot about it. But I thought I might be too small to play for

Kentucky. Georgia Southern, at that time, had a pretty good basketball program. Of course, they were well noted throughout the South for their really fine baseball program. And at the last minute, I decided (to go UK and) if I couldn't make it at Kentucky, then I can always transfer. But it worked out just fine. I wasn't afraid to work and I did work hard, and got to play a good bit in both sports at UK."

It is believed that Rupp and his aides did not even see Parsons play in high school. Yet they offered the Harlan Countian a scholarship at Kentucky.

"I don't think any of the coaches at UK even saw me play.... you know, which is unheard of," Parsons said. "They were strictly basing their opinions on what my high school coach (Gilly) was telling them. And I think they sent someone down, but it wasn't anyone on their staff. So I was fortunate to receive the opportunity to play."

Parsons said he didn't encountered any major difficulties during his freshman year at UK. Although he got homesick at times, he stayed busy by participating in basketball and baseball as well as in the classroom.

"I had a good educational background with outstanding teachers," Parsons said. "I guess though, like all youngsters who would come out of the mountains, I ended up being homesick. I guess that's pretty natural to feel that way. I've found out through the years that a lot of youngsters who come out of the mountains missed being at home. You know you're associated with such a closely-knit family. It's part of the mountain heritage and culture. But I was so busy at the time, participating in two sports and knowing the importance of a college degree and education, that I realized I needed to make that commitment. So it actually wasn't a real difficult adjustment."

Parsons was known as a consistent player who made few mistakes.

But, after seeing Parsons make a couple of errors at a practice, Rupp became angry. The coach stopped the practice and walked up to the youngster.

"Did you know that I'm writing another book?" Rupp asked.

"Well, I'm not sure but I understand that you wanted to write another book," a shaken Parsons told Rupp.

"Do you know what I'm going to entitle that book?"

"No, sir."

"Well, I'm going to entitle that book, 'What Not To Do In Basketball.' If you're not careful, all 200 pages are going to be about you."

There are many other Rupp stories, but that is one incident that Parsons will never forget. "It wasn't funny at the time, but it was funny later on," said Parsons, who once scored a career-high 21 points against Mississippi as a sophomore. "But he did get my attention. There were a lot of those kinds of stories. There are some we can repeat, but most of them we can't."

The year after Kentucky's Fiddlin' Five won the national championship, Kentucky had only one returning starter — 6-4 senior forward Johnny Cox of Hazard. The 1958-59 Wildcats had several newcomers, including 5-9 sophomore Parsons. So Rupp had a big job ahead of him. His job was to find the five best players on the floor. But the Baron often changed starting lineups throughout the season as he was not satisfied with the team's performance.

However, the surprising Wildcats did play well enough to finish with a 24-3 mark and a No. 2 national ranking. And Cox was named the first-team All-American along with Oscar Robertson of Cincinnati, Jerry West of West Virginia, Bailey Howell of Mississippi State and Bob Boozer of Kansas State.

Parsons remembers one trip late in the season when UK traveled to remote Starkville to face a dangerous Mississippi State squad. Both schools were fighting for the SEC championship.

"Life on the road was very difficult," Parsons said. "We played against Mississippi State in the old quonset hut. It looked like an airport hangar. In fact, I remember playing in there and it leaked. And it was at the time that the noise makers were allowed. They would ring those cow bells. I also remember at that time that there was a rule that had just been instituted by the conference that they couldn't ring those noise makers during free throws. Coach Rupp had told us if they would ring them, just refuse to shoot the free throws."

Late in the second half, as Kentucky prepared to shoot the free throws, the noisy Bulldog fans rang the cow bells in an attempt to rattle the visitors. So Kentucky and the officials waited for the fans to quiet down. But that didn't work.

Mississippi State coach Babe McCarthy then addressed the crowd with the public address microphone. "We're not able to ring those bells while the Kentucky players are shooting the free throws," McCarthy told the crowd. "And don't worry about it because they're going to miss them, anyway."

It was a long night. Kentucky lost 66-58, dropping its record to 18-2 for the season. Later, third-ranked Mississippi State (24-1) won the league title, but it declined to go to the NCAA tournament because it wouldn't play the integrated teams. So the Wildcats represented the 12-team conference in the NCAA.

Parsons said those incidents were "much worse than the dead skunk that they placed under our bench (at

Mississippi State two seasons later during his senior year). I was playing in the game so I didn't know a lot about that. But I understood at the time that the students would kick that skunk under the bench and we would kick it back out. It was very colorful in those days and the competition (with the Bulldogs) was quite keen."

During the late 1950s and 1960s, Rupp and McCarthy had a rivalry going in the SEC. During his 10-year stay at MSU, McCarthy compiled an overall record of 169-85 record with four SEC championships and two third-place finishes in the conference. Currently, he is the school's all-time winningest coach at Mississippi State.

After UK lost that game in Starkville in Parsons' sophomore year, it bounced back to defeat the Bulldogs in the next two seasons. In 1960, the Cats destroyed MSU 90-59 in Lexington. The 1961 contest saw Kentucky defeat the Bulldogs 68-62 in Starkville.

During the early 1960s, another point-shaving scandal hit college basketball, which had recovered from the gambling scandal of 1951. In 1961, it was learned that approximately 40 players from 22 colleges were involved in the scandal.

Unlike the 1951 gambling incident which got the Wildcats in trouble, Kentucky was not involved in the latest scandal. However, a couple of SEC schools were implicated — Tennessee and Mississippi State. All-SEC forward Jerry Graves of Mississippi State reportedly blew a game to Ole Miss for $1,500.

"They had a player named Graves and he supposedly was involved in the fix-and-shaving points (scandal)," Parsons recalled. "We always laughed about it because he made the free throws (13 out of 14) in the game (in 1961). We won that game."

In UK's 68-62 victory over host MSU, Graves had a

game-high 27 points for the Bulldogs. Roger Newman, a 6-4 senior, led the Wildcats with 24 points. Graves, who played at MSU from 1959 to '61, is currently one of the school's all-time leaders in scoring and rebounding.

Before the 1983 "Dream Game" in Knoxville, the last UK-U of L game took place in Parsons' sophomore year. In 1959, both institutions met in the Mideast Regional of the NCAA tournament in Evanston, Illinois. UK had a superb 23-2 record, while coach Peck Hickman's Louisville club was 17-10.

After losing a 15-point lead in the opening half, second-ranked Kentucky lost 76-61. The stunning victory gave unranked Louisville, which later advanced to the Final Four, a much-needed respect in college basketball. Parsons said that was probably his most disappointing moment at UK as a player.

"It seems like Louisville had more incentive to win the game," he said. "They had a very fine coaching staff. We had a very fine basketball team. It was just one of those games that when we got in trouble, we just couldn't shoot well enough to get back in the game. We were ahead 29-15 (actually 29-14) and we just ran out of gas. Louisville played well. The game didn't have the significance that it has today."

Although he performed well in basketball, Parsons had always felt that he was a better player in baseball. In 1961, the shortstop was named All-American in baseball, hitting .400 his senior year. He was also a two-time All-SEC selection (1959 and '61).

"I think it was easier for a smaller player to compete in baseball," said Parsons. "I think you see that today. There are a lot of smaller players in baseball and we had really good baseball teams at UK. To be honest, when I attended UK, I wasn't sure that I would be successful in the basketball program. But I knew if I wasn't, then I'd always have the opportunity to play baseball. That probably was my best sport.

"I think back to the days of growing up as a youngster, and how often we played baseball. In the little communities throughout southeastern Kentucky, a lot of the coal mining camps had Sunday baseball. It was semi-pro baseball and the competition was good. I had a really good background. I played a lot with older players when I was growing up and that gave me the background to develop some skills and fundamentals."

Parsons, interestingly, holds the rare honor of captaining two varsity sports at Kentucky — baseball and basketball.

Years ago, major league baseball didn't have a draft. However, Parsons and his teammate, All-SEC pitcher Charlie Loyd, were invited to play professional baseball in Georgia. They were set to play for Macon, a Class AA Southern Association club in the Los Angeles Dodgers organization, after finishing their studies at UK.

"We didn't even go through the graduation ceremonies at UK because we were planning to go on and join up with the Macon club as soon as the classes ended," Parsons said. "Max Macon was the manager and he was an SEC official. He talked to us about coming to Macon. We said that's what we would do."

But the plan fell through when Macon, the manager who was a former major league player in the 1940s, left a few days before Parsons and Loyd were scheduled to arrive in the Georgia city.

Parsons said, "Charlie did go ahead and sign with the (New York) Yankees and I had hoped maybe to get a little bonus. Washington, at the time, wanted me to come and work out. They said, 'You'll probably get your bonus if you'll just come and work out.' If I had signed with one of the clubs, I would probably have been drafted by the army. So I thought I might as well go ahead and get into teaching and coaching, which I did. I would not even had the opportunity to play baseball immediately because I'm sure I would have been drafted in the armed services."

In 1961, Parsons began his coaching career in south central Kentucky. He served as assistant football coach at Glasgow High School for a couple of years. An outstanding prep and college athlete, Parsons was no stranger in football circles. In his earlier days at Harlan High, he starred at quarterback and halfback.

Then he went to Danville where he became the head baseball and basketball coach at Boyle County High. He stayed there for five years before returning to UK.

"I never really had any good teams," Parsons recalled. "If I made a contribution, it was probably more teaching than taking a team to the state tournament (in which he was never able to accomplish) and winning a state title. But it was a fun time and there's nothing like coaching high school youngsters.

"When I received the opportunity to go back to UK, I jumped at that chance because that's where all the action was at the time."

During the 1968-69 campaign, Parsons worked on his post-graduate studies for a master's degree at UK and helped Rupp with scouting duties. Later, he became the school's head baseball coach, replacing Abe Shannon at the helm. Parsons' three-year coaching mark in baseball was 42-44-1.

In addition to his full-time baseball post, Parsons served as an assistant basketball coach on part-time basis. Parsons said Rupp invited him to join the basketball staff so that his full-time salary would be halfway decent.

Parsons is married to the former Celia Cawood of Harlan. They have two children — Ed and Kathy.

He and his wife also have four grandchildren. They enjoy spending a lot of time with them. "The fun part of having the youngsters around is that they're your grandkids and you don't have to discipline them," smiled Parsons. "You can spoil them."

And since Parsons has been out of coaching for about 15 years, he doesn't have to deal with the stress of losing games or disappointments. "My life is a little more relaxed now," he said.

Joe B. Hall, who was a former UK assistant coach before replacing Adolph Rupp as the school's head coach in 1972, is shown with his 1969-70 scholarship freshman players. Pictured, from left to right, are Glenn Sims (student manager), Doug Flynn, Steve Penhorwood, Larry Stamper, Dan Perry, Jim Andrews and Hall.

University of Kentucky Media Relations Office

Dick Parsons, a former longtime assistant under Adolph Rupp and Joe B. Hall, said the coaching staff once hid future All-American Kevin Grevey in Lexington from other college recruiters.

Photo by Jamie H. Vaught

Ex-Kentucky head coach Eddie Sutton gives instructions to senior guard Roger Harden during a game at Rupp Arena in the 1985-86 campaign. Kentucky finished that season with a superb 32-4 mark and a No. 3 national ranking by the Associated Press.

Photo by Jamie H. Vaught, *Commonwealth Journal*

Former UK player Chris Gettelfinger and his wife, Jill, are relaxing with their cat at the couple's Knoxville home in Tennessee.

Photo by Jamie H. Vaught

Bernadette Locke-Mattox in her younger days at the University of Georgia. Notice her knee-high socks. The Wildcat players and coaches later teased her about these knee-high socks at a practice while she served as an assistant for Rick Pitino.

University of Georgia
Sports Information Office

Jim Master talks with his client on the phone in his Lexington office. The former Wildcat guard almost signed with Notre Dame, his hometown school, in 1980 before he changed his mind.

Photo by Jamie H. Vaught

John Pelphrey, now an assistant coach at Marshall University, says
his most difficult moment at Kentucky came when the NCAA imposed
near-death penalty sanctions on the school in 1989. In 1991-92,
Pelphrey was one of the four seniors — popularly called "The
Unforgettables" — who helped the Wildcats restore their winning
tradition.

Photo by Chris Jones

Former UK All-American Frank Ramsey is pictured in his Webster County office where he serves as the president of Dixon Bank.

Photo by Jamie H. Vaught

Ex-Boston Celtics coach Red Auerbach (shown with his trademark cigar) and Kentucky's Adolph Rupp were both "dictators," according to Frank Ramsey, who played for both legendary figures.

Boston Celtics
Public Relations Department

Larry Conley, shown at left with his broadcasting partner Paul Kennedy during a regional SEC telecast, describes Adolph Rupp as "a powerful man." The former Kentucky star also comments that the news media, especially on the national level, haven't been fair in their generally-unfavorable portrayal of Rupp.

Photo by Jamie H. Vaught

Boxing great Muhammad Ali appeared at the 1995 Kentucky-Florida game at Rupp Arena, sitting on the bench with the Wildcats. He poses with Christopher Pitino, son of Rick Pitino, during the halftime of UK's 87-77 victory over the Gators.

Photo by Jamie H. Vaught

Rival coach Denny Crum of Louisville isn't happy with the official's call as he argues in the Cardinals' 71-64 victory over Kentucky at Louisville's Freedom Hall in 1984. One of the nation's winningest coaches, Crum, however, hasn't been very successful against Kentucky since both schools started to play each other in 1983. Entering the 1995-96 season, Crum's all-time coaching record against the Cats is 5-9.

Photo by Jamie H. Vaught,
Commonwealth Journal

Star forward James Lee, a product of Henry Clay High School, is shown in his pre-Rupp Arena days at UK's Memorial Coliseum. Notice his low-cut Converse basketball shoes.

Photo by David Rogers

Rick Pitino has guided the Wildcats to 22 or more victories every season since he was hired in 1989 with the exception of his probation-ridden first Kentucky squad which finished at 14-14. Pitino — who has captured four straight SEC tournament crowns and made four consecutive NCAA tournament appearances, including the 1993 Final Four — enters his seventh year at the UK helm in the 1995-96 campaign.

Photo by David Rogers

Kentucky Basketball great
Cotton Nash, shown in early
1960s, is one of the few athletes
who have played major league
baseball and pro basketball.

University of Kentucky Media
Relations Office

Then-Kentucky senior Winston
Bennett, a Louisville native,
goes up for two points against
arch-rival U of L as the
Wildcats won the nationally-
televised thriller by a score of
76-75 during the 1987-88 season.   Senior teammate Rob
Lock looks on.

Photo by Chris Jones

Joanne Pitino, wife of UK roundball mentor, and C. M. Newton listen to Rick Pitino's remarks at a press conference in 1989 when UK officially hired the New Yorker as its new head coach.

Photo by Jamie H. Vaught

C. M. Newton and Wendell Hudson — shown in 1978 as head coach and assistant coach, respectively, at Alabama — have enjoyed a special relationship. Hudson, the first black to earn a basketball scholarship for the Crimson Tide, played and coached under Newton. Hudson encountered difficult times during the late 1960s and the early 1970s when there were some racial problems in the South, Newton says.

University of Alabama Sports Information Office

NATIONAL BASKETBALL ASSOCIATION

UNIFORM PLAYER CONTRACT

THIS AGREEMENT made this ninth day of April 19 62 by and between Chicago Attractions, Inc.
(hereinafter called the Club), a member of the National Basketball Association, and Larry Pursiful
of the City, Town of _____ (hereinafter called the Player).

WITNESSETH:—

In consideration of the several and/or mutual promises and/or agreements hereinafter contained, the parties hereto promise and agree as follows:

1. The Club hereby employs the Player as a skilled Basketball Player for the term of one year from the 1st day of October 19 The Player's employment shall include attendance at training camp, playing the games scheduled for the team during the schedule season of the National Basketball Association, playing all exhibition games scheduled by the team during and prior to the schedule season, and playing the playoff games for which the player is to receive such additional compensation as is provided by the Association. Regular players will not be required to attend training camp earlier than four weeks prior to the season starting date of the team of which the player is a member. "Rookies" may be required to attend training camp at an earlier date. Exhibition games shall not be played on the three days prior to the opening of a team's regular season schedule nor on a day prior to a regularly scheduled game. The All-Star game shall for the purpose of this paragraph not be considered an exhibition game. Exhibition games during the regularly scheduled season shall not exceed three.

2. The club agrees to pay the Player for rendering services described herein the sum of $ 7000.00 in twelve equal semi-monthly payments beginning with the first of said payments on November 15th of the season above described and continuing with such payments on the first and fifteenth of each month until said sum is paid in full. Provided however if the Club does not qualify for the playoffs the payments due subsequent to the conclusion of the schedule season shall become due and payable immediately after the conclusion of the schedule season.

3. The Club promises and agrees to pay the reasonable board and lodging expenses of the Player while playing for the Club in other than the Club's home city and will pay all proper and necessary expenses of the Player and his meals enroute. Each basketball player, while "on the road," shall be paid seven dollars ($7.00) per day as meal expense allowance.

4. The club may from time to time during the continuance of this contract establish reasonable rules for the government of its players "at home" and "abroad," and such rules shall be a part of this contract as fully as if herein written and shall be binding upon the player; and for violation of such rules or for any conduct impairing the faithful and thorough discharge of the duties incumbent upon the player, the club may impose reasonable fines upon the player and deduct the amount thereof from any money due or to become due to the player. The club may also suspend the player for violation of any rules so established, and during such suspension the player shall not be entitled to any compensation under this contract. When the player is fined or suspended, he shall be given notice in writing, stating the amount of the fine or the duration of the suspension and the reason therefor.

4a. During the term of this contract the Player will not cause or take part in any strike (whether sit-down, sympathetic, general or of any other nature), walk-out, picketing, boycotting (whether primary or secondary), or fail, refuse or neglect faithfully to discharge his duties hereunder or encourage or cause any other player under contract to the Club or to any other club which is a member of the National Basketball Association to fail, refuse or neglect faithfully to discharge his duties thereunder, or interfere in any manner whatsoever with the operation or conduct of the business of the said Association or of any member thereof. For any violation of this Paragraph 4a, the Club and the President of the said Association shall each have the concurrent right and power to terminate this contract forthwith, to fine the Player, to suspend him for a definite or an indefinite period, and /or to impose upon him such other disciplinary action as the Club or the President of the said Association shall deem appropriate, and the President of the said Association shall have the additional right and power in his sole discretion to expel the Player, or to suspend him for a definite or an indefinite period, as a player for any member of the said Association. The Club shall have the right to deduct from any money due or to become due to the Player the amount of any fine imposed hereunder and the Player shall not be entitled to any compensation under this contract during the period of any suspension hereunder. Any fine or suspension hereunder shall be imposed by notice in writing delivered or mailed to the Player, stating the amount of the fine, the duration of the suspension and the reason therefor and the Player shall be entitled to no other notice or hearing in connection therewith.

5. The Player promises and agrees (a) to report at the time and place fixed by the Club in good physical condition; and (b) to keep himself throughout the entire season in good physical condition; and (c) to give his best services, as well as his loyalty, to the Club, and to play basketball only for the Club unless released, sold or exchanged by the Club; and (d) to be neatly and fully attired in public and always to conduct himself on and off the court according to the highest standards of honesty, morality, fair play and sports-

A partial copy of ex-UK star Larry Pursiful's NBA contract for a $7,000 salary. He never did sign the pact.

Courtesy Larry Pursiful

Larry Pursiful, a former All-SEC player at UK, says Adolph Rupp used to fuss at him for not shooting enough baskets.

Photo by Jamie H. Vaught

(Below) Ex-UK All-American Kenny Walker (34) attempts to shoot over Mississippi State's Tony Robinson as teammate Bret Bearup watches in UK's narrow 58-57 win in 1985. That season marked coach Joe B. Hall's last year at Kentucky.

Photo by Jamie H. Vaught, *Commonwealth Journal*

10 Masterful Cat

JIM MASTER

Jim Master was just barely 18 years old when he made one of the most important decisions of his life.

A highly-celebrated prep superstar from Fort Wayne, Indiana, who made the prestigious McDonald's and Parade All-American teams, he chose Kentucky over Notre Dame, Purdue and Ohio State in the spring of 1980. He liked the school's rich basketball history. He liked the Wildcat players. He liked coach Joe B. Hall and his assistants, especially Joe Dean Jr. He just liked Kentucky the best.

By becoming a Wildcat, he joined an impressive list of prep stars from the Hoosier state — Cliff Barker, Louie Dampier, Mike Flynn, Kyle Macy, to name a few — who have played for coaches Adolph Rupp and Joe B. Hall at UK.

The decision actually was a big relief. For him and his parents. He had been under tremendous pressure to stay home and play basketball in the state of Indiana.

Master said most of the pressure to stay home came from the Purdue fans. Purdue, by the way, was coached by Kentuckian Lee Rose, who took the Boilermakers to the 1980 NCAA Final Four and the coach had made a good impression on the youngster.

"(Rose) was the only reason I was probably interested in Purdue," Master said in an interview at his Lexington office where he is an investment broker.

But Purdue actually wasn't at the top of his list. He was more interested in other schools in the state — Indiana and Notre Dame. These programs had well-known, established coaches in Bobby Knight and Digger Phelps.

"I was interested in Indiana, but they had Isiah Thomas," explained Master. "So, it wasn't that interested."

On Notre Dame, that was his favorite team in Indiana. He had dreams of playing for the Fighting Irish. He grew up a big Notre Dame fan and liked Phelps. In fact, the night before he announced his college choice, he was leaning toward the Irish, who had a future All-American guard by the name of John Paxson. As it turned out, Notre Dame was his second choice behind Kentucky.

"I grew up (in Plymouth) about 20 miles south of South Bend and that's where Notre Dame is," said Master who played at Plymouth High before transferring to Fort Wayne's Paul Harding High after his sophomore year. "I grew up emulating Notre Dame players. Just like the Kentucky kids growing up in Kentucky and wanting to play for Kentucky."

Growing up, Master was never a fan of UK. He didn't follow the Wildcats. "When you're young up in northern Indiana, usually you have Indiana, Purdue and Notre Dame," he said. "So Notre Dame and Indiana were the teams I followed pretty closely. I'm a big-time Notre Dame fan.

"I was real good friends with John Paxson on that team. I liked him a lot. He was one of the reasons I could've gone to Notre Dame. But, then again, we may have played a similar position, even though he was more of a point guard, and a good one.

"I really liked Digger Phelps a lot. Of course, some of the other players who played for him said he was hard to play for in some ways, but he put a lot of players in the pros. I really liked his flamboyant attitude. Real outgoing. I was really impressed."

When Master made up his mind about college, he had a difficult time in talking to Phelps on the phone. He tearfully informed the coach that he was going to Kentucky.

And when the player contacted UK, Dean was the one who took the call as Hall was out of town on a fishing trip. Dean had doubts that he would hear the good news, figuring Master was heading for Notre Dame. The stunned assistant coach was extremely elated with Master's decision.

Over a decade later, Phelps — who once said that coaching basketball at UK was like coaching football at hot-bed Notre Dame — resigned from his Notre Dame job after the 1990-91 season. The ex-coach is doing some television work on ESPN cable network today. One of the most outspoken persons in the coaching profession, Phelps openly discussed many issues in college basketball.

"I've followed his career pretty much so I'm very familiar with what he's done and some of things he stands for outside of sports," Master said. "I'm more impressed with him (about his views) as opposed to just being a coach at Notre Dame. I've listened to a lot of interviews. I think he cared about the education of his athletes."

Before making his college choice, Master — who also received highly-acclaimed Indiana's "Mr. Basketball" honors after his senior year in high school — had conversations with Macy, the ex-UK star who grew up in the cities of Fort Wayne and Peru in Indiana. Ironically, it's Macy whom many people compared Master with. They both were sharpshooters. They were from the same state. They were nice-looking prep All-Americans.

"I talked to Kyle since we were from basically the same geographical location and he was (Indiana's) Mr.

Basketball and I was Mr. Basketball," Master recalled. "I discussed it with him before I made my decision. But I actually did it with a lot of people. So I think I did a thorough job for an 18-year-old kid, trying to make my mind up where I wanted to go."

As a 6-4, 165-pound senior at Paul Harding High, he averaged nearly 28 points, shooting 52 percent of his field goal attempts and 89 percent of his free throws. His coach, Harlan Frick, said Master reminded him of Indiana native Rick Mount, the former Purdue star. Master shot the ball as well as any high school player he has ever seen, according to Frick.

Master said the pressure to perform that he would later face at Kentucky did not concern him.

"That really never entered the picture at all," he commented. "There was going to be pressure wherever I went."

Like any other player, Master had ups and downs during his four-year career at Kentucky.

He had several good moments. He made All-SEC teams twice (1982 and '83). Like a true veteran guard with lots of poise, he played extremely well in the 1983 "Dream Game" against Louisville in Knoxville, making only two turnovers and scoring 18 points, including a key basket which sent the game into overtime. He helped the Wildcats to a Final Four appearance in 1984 as a senior. And, while at UK, the Cats compiled a 96-27 overall record, including four NCAA tournament trips.

The bad moments. Losing to rival U of L in the "Dream Game." Dropping to Georgetown in the 1984 Final Four on UK's atrocious 3-for-33 field goal shooting in the second half. Missing curfews. Stormy relationship with coach Joe B. Hall. Losing first-round NCAA tournament games for two consecutive years.

Master said his senior year was not a complete success. Besides Master, the 1983-84 Wildcats had Sam Bowie, Melvin Turpin, Kenny Walker, Winston Bennett, Dicky Beal, Bret Bearup, to name a few. Although they finished with an outstanding 29-5 mark, the Wildcats should've done better, according to Master.

"We thought maybe we should have lost only one or two games," he said. "Even though it was a great year in a lot of ways, it was very disappointing in other ways. We had so much talent and I think it was disappointing to all of us to even lose five games that year. The way the season ended with the Georgetown game was very disappointing."

What happened in UK's ugly 53-40 setback to Georgetown at Seattle's Kingdome after leading 29-22 at the halftime? There were several reasons, Master said.

"We had high expectations to really be like a 32-2 team or something like that, but we ran into a tough team," Master explained. "We ran into a different style of ball at the time. Georgetown was very physical and that's kind of what I think ended up swaying the game more towards their favor. And we just never could recuperate, we never could get back into the flow.

"Georgetown was a great team and they had a great defense. Patrick Ewing was probably the best defensive player, not only in college basketball, but maybe in the world at that time. The roughness and the physicalness of their style and playing in a huge arena (were also factors).

"We started out well and we mentally were thinking it was going to be easy after we were ahead seven, eight, nine points in the middle of the first half. Everything came easy at first and then they clamped down. I don't think we ever got back into the flow."

A year earlier in 1983, Master also played in the NCAA tournament. Before advancing to the Mideast Regional finals for a "Dream Game" with Louisville, the hot-shooting Wildcats defeated Indiana and 7-2 center Uwe Blab 64-59, hitting 63 percent of their field goals.

Junior center Melvin Turpin paced the Wildcat attack with 16 points.

After the victory over the Hoosiers on a Thursday night, Master and his teammates did not stay around at Stokely Athletics Center to watch the Louisville-Arkansas game in the nightcap.

"We watched the game in the Holiday Inn down there in Knoxville," Master said. "We didn't see it live. We were back in our rooms watching it. Louisville made a dramatic comeback and won."

Then came the wild hoopla. The long-awaited "Dream Game" had finally arrived. Kentucky and Louisville were to play each other for the first time in many years. And even Kentucky Gov. John Y. Brown Jr. got excited in the affair. He wore a blue and red sportscoat at the game, showing off the school colors for both teams. The news media was everywhere and the CBS television network, with roundball junkie Billy Packer, was carrying the matchup.

"The excitement all around the hotel for the next two days was pretty amazing," Master said. "I think all the players, if they were to think back, would probably say that was the most exciting time (of their Wildcat careers). That was probably the biggest hype and most excitement which we played in, including the Final Four when we went (in 1984)."

Master, a junior, was very impressive in the Louisville game. For UK, playing without injured star Sam Bowie, he was perhaps the best player it had that afternoon.

Facing a tough defense, Master hit nine of 13 baskets for 18 points, which tied him for team lead with Turpin. And in 40 minutes of action, he committed only two miscues. For his tourney efforts, he was named to the Mideast All-Regional team. However, it wasn't enough as the Cardinals prevailed 80-68 in overtime.

Although he had a good performance individually, Master said that was probably the most disappointing game of his UK career because "we were that close to making it into the Final Four." After the loss, he had tears in his eyes. But at the same time, it was Master's "most exciting game I've been associated with. Whoever won that game was going to the Final Four. It was an emotional game. We played hard. We were close (to winning), but we fell apart in the overtime. The press (defense) got us. It was very tough for the players to get over it. It was a great game for 40 minutes. We gave it our best shot and just didn't win it. They were probably a little better than us that year, but we still didn't have Bowie. We had some nice players."

In beating Kentucky, Louisville traveled to picturesque Albuquerque, New Mexico, for the big Final Four party. But U of L dropped to Houston's Phi Slama Jama kids, including Akeem (now Hakeem) Olajuwon, 94-81, in the semifinals, finishing its season with a 32-4 worksheet. And it was that Final Four when North Carolina State coach Jim Valvano excitedly ran on the court, looking for someone to hug, after his Cinderella squad (26-10) captured the 1983 national championship.

It is a well-known fact that coach Joe B. Hall didn't want to play Louisville. But what about the Wildcat players? Were they in favor of playing the Cardinals?

"I think most players want to play against great teams," Master said. "Obviously, they (the Cardinals) were a great team at the time. You always want to play those teams as opposed to someone else. And the players like the hype and they like the big-game atmosphere. Obviously you don't get much of a bigger game, at that time, than Kentucky-Louisville. So, yeah, I'm sure we were in favor of it.

"Joe Hall felt that by playing the teams in the state (UK) had nothing to win and everything to lose. I think there's some good thought process to that theory. It's a reality that University of Kentucky has many more fans inside the state. There are a lot of teams around the country who don't play their in-state rival if they're perceived as being the big honcho or the big kid on the block. So I really don't have a problem with both sides. I can see both arguments at that time.

"As players, though, you didn't care who you played as long as it was an Indiana or a North Carolina. You wanted to play the good teams. You didn't enjoy playing the teams which weren't the marquee names because I really do think you had nothing to gain and everything to lose."

In Master's freshman and sophomore seasons at Kentucky, the Wildcats didn't go very far. Shockingly, they were knocked out in the first round of the NCAA tournament by Alabama-Birmingham and Middle Tennessee State. Out of the NCAA tournament early in two straight years? Unthinkable, said the angry Wildcat fans after second early knockout.

"That was a disaster," Master said of the 1981 and '82 tournaments. "I don't think you could make any excuses. It was so bad. That was tough, I'm telling you. That was about the low point in UK basketball, I think. I don't know what else to tell you. It was embarrassing. I still hate to think about it."

Did Master feel sorry for Hall, who was roundly criticized for losing those two games? Some say he couldn't coach anymore. The game had just passed him by, they said.

"I didn't have time to feel sorry for him," said Master, who led the SEC with an 89.6 free throw percentage in 1982. "Probably us, yeah."

Of the two, the 50-44 setback to a scrappy Middle Tennessee State team in 1982 at Nashville was the worse one. Kentucky — which had Derrick Hord, Master, Turpin and Dirk Minniefield as the team's leading scorers — was clearly a giant favorite over the Ohio Valley Conference school, but it somehow couldn't make the baskets at the end when it counted the most. Kentucky hit only four points in the last 13 minutes of the game. Perhaps the Wildcats looked ahead to a date with Louisville, which they hadn't played against for many years.

"The Middle Tennessee State (game) was probably the most embarrassing and the toughest one since Alabama-Birmingham was coming along at that time," commented Master, who gunned in eight points against the Blue Raiders.

The previous year had seen the newly-established Alabama-Birmingham — which was in its third year of basketball competition — upset a Sam Bowie-led Kentucky team. Earlier, the Blazers had just captured their first-ever NCAA tournament matchup against Western Kentucky 93-68 before facing UK. UAB's 69-62 tourney victory over the Wildcats avenged its earlier loss to Kentucky in the regular season. (In the now-defunct UKIT, the Wildcats had beaten UAB, coached by former UCLA mentor Gene Bartow, 61-53 for their Christmas tourney title.)

While at UK, Master said he never considered leaving the Wildcats. Even when the times were hard. Even when he had problems with the coach. Even when he missed the curfews.

"I missed two curfews that I can remember," he said. "I was always your typical young man at that time. (Guard) Troy McKinley was with me one time. All of us got into trouble another time. (Someone) came to check on us after a game that we had won and 10 out of 12 of us were still out."

What was the penalty?

"We had to get up about 6:00 in the morning and run," Master recalled. "Some of the players were still not in even at 6:00. So later they had to run after practice. But we got scolded pretty well. And if you missed a class, you got in trouble. The discipline was there, but boys will be boys. I got suspended for one game for breaking curfew and didn't play. I've gotten into some trouble, just not coming in on curfew. So when we get together, everybody laughs at the times they got caught. More so than when we talk about the times we won ballgames."

Master's one-game suspension occurred during his senior year when he, along with McKinley, sat out the UK-Ole Miss contest in Oxford. "I went down there and didn't play," said Master. A struggling Kentucky team won the game anyway, beating the Rebels 68-55 as his replacement, freshman guard James Blackmon, made a team-high 15 points. That game marked Blackmon's first collegiate start.

Before Master received the word that he was being suspended, coach Joe B. Hall had called the player into his office. Master remembers the meeting.

"Well, he might not want me to tell you that he was smoking a cigar," recalled the ex-Wildcat. "(He was) saying, 'You broke curfew but I've decided to take you on the trip.' I remember those times when he was yelling and screaming at me for missing curfew."

Also, earlier in his UK career, Master got into an argument with Hall which cost him a starting role in a 56-51 loss to Mississippi State in Starkville during the 1981-82 season. It would be the only game he did not start that year as he started in the team's other 29 games.

"I was suspended for talking back to him in my sophomore year," Master said. "He took me on the trip. I didn't start, (but) I played."

Master admits that his relationship with Hall wasn't a bed of roses. It was partly because of his lack of maturity, he said. He has no one to blame but himself.

"Boys will be boys," Master said. "Our relationship was stormy, but I think most of the players' relationships with him were. I think, in some parts, he even wanted it that way. I think he was from the old Adolph Rupp school and he didn't care if the players liked him or not. That didn't bother me. Now, I'm really good friends with him. But back then it was very stormy."

During the eight-game Japan exhibition tour in the summer of 1982, Hall was almost a different person, according to Master. He was easy going despite the fact the trip came after the season had ended with that infamous Middle Tennessee State fiasco in the NCAA tournament.

"Joe Hall was good to us, meaning he didn't care as long as it wasn't illegal," Master said. "He didn't really put a curfew on us. We could do about whatever we wanted to do as long as we showed up for the games.

"We had a lot of good alumni with us. It was really a great 22-day trip. The basketball experience was secondary to just the experience of going to a new culture with all your friends and a lot of people you hang around with."

Master, who has a business degree from UK, has seen Rick Pitino coach on the sidelines. Does he think Hall was more demanding than Pitino is now? Master isn't sure.

"Well, I don't know, but I think both of them are pretty good disciplinarians," he said. "Joe Hall was. He made us go to class and kept a pretty tight fist on us. He was pretty good at making curfews, requiring coat and tie and no facial hair — that type of things. (He ran) pretty much by the book. He wanted you to act a certain way, but that was good. I think he did a lot of good things, disciplinary-wise."

Although Hall has won eight SEC titles and made three trips to the NCAA Final Four, including a national championship in 1978, some demanding fans have said the former mentor didn't do enough at Kentucky. What about the other coaches? Many of them were or are in a similar situation.

What about LSU coach Dale Brown, the so-called "Dean of SEC Basketball Coaches," whom Master had faced several times while at UK? Master has a theory about outspoken Brown, who has sent the Tigers to the Final Four twice in his long tenure at the Baton Rouge school.

"I just don't think he's been as successful as he should have been down there just because he's had some unbelievable talent," he reasoned.

Kentucky versus Notre Dame.

UK's rivalry with the Fighting Irish meant a lot to Master. His feelings of affection for Notre Dame, his hometown school, ran very deep in his heart.

"It was pretty special," Master said of the series.

He and his Wildcat teammates faced Notre Dame three times and they won two of them. However, Master's first game as a Wildcat against the Irish wasn't memorable. UK lost that game, 67-61, in 1980.

The next one wasn't all that good, either. Although the Cats won the game in overtime at Louisville, it was ugly. A very low-scoring affair. The final score was 34-28 as Notre Dame held the ball, angering a pro-Wildcat crowd of nearly 17,000.

"It was real disappointing," Master said of the stall. "I didn't like that. That was a bummer."

He was very surprised that coach Digger Phelps, who had junior guard John Paxson, decided to use the "slow-ball" strategy against UK, Master said.

Then, in the second game of the 1982-83 season, UK posted a 58-45 victory over the Irish at South Bend. It was Master's last game against Notre Dame, and both of his parents and several relatives saw him play.

"The third one was the most memorable one

because we hadn't played up in there in forever and ever, and we beat them pretty good," Master said. "It was special. We played really well."

That game marked the Cats' first appearance at South Bend since 1950 and the end of a long-running series. But the series was revived as both schools met in Louisville in 1988 under then-UK coach Eddie Sutton's regime.

By the way, Master later covered the 1990 Kentucky-Notre Dame game in South Bend as a TV analyst for the UK network.

In 1980, both Master and 6-9 forward Bret Bearup came to Kentucky at the same time as highly-regarded freshmen. They were outgoing and became very close friends. Bearup loved doing crazy things, pulling pranks on his teammates. And both of them sometimes got into trouble for clowning around too far.

"Bearup's the one who used to pull all the jokes," Master said. "We had shaving cream fights in the (Wildcat) Lodge and got into trouble for that. We were always really having fun with each other. All the players were."

Bearup recalled one prank he pulled on Master early in their freshman year during the Christmas holidays. Bearup got a dead chicken from a local farm after a dog had just killed it. After grabbing the chicken away from the dog, he took the dead creature back to the UK campus.

"(I) put it under Jim Master's bed," Bearup said. "He and Dicky Beal had the same room. That night we left for the Notre Dame game. We didn't come back for two days. When we came back, they opened the door...oh, did it stink to high heaven in there! They didn't know what in the world it was."

And, while Bearup was out, Master got his revenge by placing the dead chicken in his friend's closet. But the battle wasn't over as Bearup later hung the chicken outside by the windows where Master and Beal lived.

"I know the next morning when he (Beal) opened the blind, there was that dead chicken staring him right in the face," Bearup smiled, adding Beal liked to get up in the morning and open the windows to get some fresh air.

Said former UK assistant coach Joe Dean Jr., "Bret was a prankster.... He was always involved in mischief and things. I think one time he went a little too far and coach Hall got after him."

At Kentucky, Master and star teammate Sam Bowie were also good buddies. They still keep in touch with each other, despite the fact they lived in separate cities for many years during the roundball season as Bowie was playing in the NBA.

"Bowie and I were pretty close," Master said. "He has been a close friend for a long time. I visited him in Los Angeles, New Jersey and Portland where he played. He lives here in town (Lexington) during the off-season and we play golf. I was in his wedding several years ago and they've got a nice, good-looking young child (Samantha)."

Bowie and his wife, Heidi, have been married for several years. They began dating while Bowie was a high school senior in Pennsylvania.

After his senior year, Master was drafted in the sixth round by NBA's Atlanta Hawks. His three other teammates — Bowie (first round), Melvin Turpin (first round) and Beal (fourth round) — were also picked in the 1984 draft. It was The Draft which had North Carolina star Michael Jordan, who went to Chicago as the league's third pick overall.

Master, a member of UK's exclusive 1,000-point

club with 1,283 points, was realistic about his pro chances. He didn't have high expectations, but he was going to try out. He had nothing to lose.

"I had a good tryout," he said. "That was fun. I also tried out with the Pacers. I knew I didn't have a good chance back then. You got to be drafted high (to make it) and that was okay. All of these great players were trying to make the team, knowing that probably only one out of about 20 of them were going to make the team because of guaranteed contracts (held by the veterans). I'm glad I had that experience. It's tough to make those teams so it didn't (bother me). It was a great experience. I don't begrudge it at all."

That was the end of his basketball playing career. Unlike several former UK players, Master didn't play pro basketball overseas. He moved on to the business world.

His parents — Paul and Sandy Master — were the biggest fans Master had at UK. They practically attended every UK game — home and away. They just loved to watch their youngest child play. They also have three other children — two sons and a daughter. A close family, Master said.

"They were big supporters," Master said of his mother and father. "I don't think they missed a game. They traveled and watched me play."

That included conference games with the Florida Gators in Gainesville which was about a thousand miles away from their home in northern Indiana.

"My dad owned a little property down there (in Florida)," said the younger Master. "He had a pretty lenient job and a lot of vacation time. He's worked for the same company forever."

Paul Master worked for the telephone company. He recently retired from the firm. His mother is a housewife. They are busy with "grandchildren and stuff. Not from me," said the younger Master, who admitted that he would like to get married and have kids someday.

Several years after his Wildcat playing days ended, Master — who also wrote syndicated columns for several newspapers in the state — began his broadcasting career.

In 1989, which was coach Rick Pitino's first year at UK, Master became the color commentator for the UK Basketball Television Network, joining play-by-play announcer Ralph Hacker. He was chosen for the position over three ex-UK standouts — Jay Shidler, Jimmy Dan Conner and Rick Robey. Earlier, some thought Master had hurt his chances for the job when he publicly said that the Wildcats need a coaching change when embattled Eddie Sutton was the head coach.

"I wanted to stay close to the game," Master said of his TV job. "I just thought I could do it and basically went to Ralph Hacker and Jim Host and told them that I'd like an opportunity to do it. That's how I got started.

"It kept me close to the game for a few years, when you still wanted to be close to the game, but you couldn't play. I think I did two years on the UK network, but I was doing some radio and stuff for different people. I did the Ohio Valley Conference for one year. I enjoyed it. I think I did pretty good at it. It was fun to stay close to the game during that time."

In addition to his UK network job, Master also had a couple of assignments with Jefferson-Pilot on its SEC Game-of-the-Week regional telecasts. "That was an experience," Master commented. "I'm glad I got to do it."

Call him a Masterful Cat, the one who has successfully mastered his skills in a variety of jobs.

11 | Sir Winston

WINSTON BENNETT

Shortly after Rick Pitino hired him to be an assistant coach at Kentucky, Winston Bennett was reading a best-selling book during the summer of 1994. No, he didn't read a summer romance novel to kill some dead time. Actually, in preparing for his new job, he analyzed the book — written by former New York Knicks coach Pat Riley — like a serious graduate student doing a research paper.

In reading Riley's *The Winner Within*, Bennett became fascinated with what the author/coach discussed about building success in workplace as well as personal life. "He has so much experience (to share with)," said Bennett, a former UK star who played three years in the NBA.

Although they have faced against each other in pro basketball, Bennett does not know Riley. "I never met him personally," said a well-mannered Bennett. "I have played against his teams a couple of times."

Before accepting his current coaching post at UK, Bennett had been working at a bank in Louisville, his hometown. At PNC Bank, he served as a credit analyst and was training to be a commercial loan officer. In the early 1990s, Bennett started his new career in banking after suffering a serious knee injury which forced him to quit pro basketball.

On his banking career, "That was a tremendous experience for me because I was learning things that I didn't know a whole lot about before. But, after a year of doing that, I really got the feeling that my passion was still in the game of basketball."

So Bennett stayed in touch in basketball circles. During the 1993-94 season, he worked as a commentator for the UK Radio Network, covering the Wildcat games. Since he still lived in Louisville, he commuted back and forth to work the Wildcat games in Lexington and on the road. But he still had dreams of coaching on either college or pro level someday.

In the spring of 1994, when Pitino called and told the former Wildcat that he got the job, Bennett became excited with his promising basketball future. "I was very elated," he said. "A lot went into the decision being made for me to come on the coaching staff — a lot of prayers from my parents, myself and my immediate family. I was very excited about it and it is certainly a tremendous honor to be a part of this staff.

"I thought that by pursuing a coaching opportunity this would not only get me close to the game, it would also get me where I love doing and helping kids reach their potential. A way to stay in the game is to teach the game. Teach young people what it takes to be champions, what it takes to pursue excellence in the game of basketball."

For Bennett, coaching at his alma mater is basically a dream come true. "Kentucky basketball is the ultimate basketball experience," he said. "If basketball players go to heaven when they die, this is the heaven."

But Bennett's new paycheck took a dive. His coaching job, at the time, was classified as a "restricted-earnings" position, which meant an annual salary of $16,000, including $4,000 from basketball summer camps.

In 1995, a federal judge struck down the position, ruling the NCAA had broken the antitrust laws by placing salary limits for the restricted-earnings coaches.

While working at the bank, he earned a more comfortable salary. "A pay cut is not even close," Bennett said of his first-year coaching salary. "A tremendous pay cut is more like it."

Pitino said Bennett reminded him of Stu Jackson, his former assistant who later became the head coach of the New York Knicks. The UK mentor said Bennett has same qualities that Jackson had — a great future and a great presence.

Bennett stated that he wasn't really worried about his lack of coaching experience when he applied for the coaching position.

"It didn't concern me at all," he said. "I felt that I was willing to work hard enough to get that experience once I get there. If coach Pitino was willing to give me the opportunity, then I would be willing to do the rest as far as being a sponge to absorb any information that comes along the information highway, so to speak."

A quiet, conscientious person, Bennett said no one individual has really encouraged him to enter the coaching profession. But the ex-Wildcat said he "got my inspiration from the Lord. He has funny ways of showing you things as you go through life. I don't think any one person told me that coaching would be a great thing for me."

During the exciting 1994-95 campaign, Bennett learned the ropes and saw his deep and talented squad go all the way to the NCAA final eight. Although the second-ranked Cats, led by dependable 6-1 guard Tony Delk, were a heavy Final Four favorite, they completed the 28-5 season on a disappointing note with a 13-point setback to North Carolina in the Southeast Regional finals.

In the UK basketball camp, as this book was written, there were discussions that Bennett was expected to do some coaching for Kentucky's newly-revived junior varsity squad in the 1995-96 season.

While at Louisville Male High School in the early 1980s, the 6-7 Bennett was a starter all four years and became a highly-regarded prep superstar. As a senior, he averaged 25.4 points and 11.9 rebounds in guiding Male to the 7th Region finals with a 29-3 record and was named to nearly every high school All-American team. In addition, he was chosen Kentucky's "Mr. Basketball" in 1983.

And the state's two biggest universities — Kentucky and Louisville — sought his playing services. The rivals recruited him very hard. Joe B. Hall wanted him. Denny Crum wanted him.

Since Bennett lived in Louisville, there was a lot of pressure for him to sign with the Cardinals.

"They wanted to see a young man in Louisville's backyard stay home and play for the University of Louisville," Bennett said. "I can respect that, but I felt I owed it to myself and my family to check out the alternatives — to see what could be a better alternative than going to the University of Louisville and I found that at UK."

Even though Louisville recruited him fiercely, Bennett never really was very interested in playing for Crum and the Cards. Kentucky, by far, was his favorite school.

"As long as Kentucky was in the picture, there wasn't a chance that I was going to attend Louisville," Bennett said. "(I don't want) to put a black cloud over Louisville because Louisville has one of the best programs in the country. I have a lot of respect for coach Denny Crum. As you can see, Louisville won two championships in the 1980s. If I had attended there, maybe I would be wearing championship rings. But certainly there is never a doubt (about his college decision). If I had to make the decision over again, I would certainly choose Kentucky. It was the best scenario for me."

So Bennett became the first player from Louisville to sign with Kentucky in more than a decade. Hall and his assistant, Leonard Hamilton, did most of the recruiting for Kentucky. Bennett's first impression of Hall?

"A strong man," Bennett recalled. "One who embodied discipline out of his players. One who wanted the best out of his players. He wanted his players to excel both on and off the court.

Hall's reputation as a tough disciplinarian "didn't scare me because I come from a disciplined home," Bennett said. "My parents are both disciplined people. They were not overly strict but they wanted certain things done certain ways. Some things they believe in, some things they don't. I grew up in the church. I am an only child. My father owns his carpet cleaning business and my mother is a housewife."

Joe B. Hall and Denny Crum were not the only people wanting to sign Bennett.

How about coach Bobby Knight of Indiana? He liked Bennett, too. He visited the player and his parents in Louisville.

"After talking for hours, he asked me where was I going to go to school and I told him that I wasn't going to Indiana," Bennett said. "He wanted to know why not. He said they had the best program and on and on. I just said that I didn't want to go to Indiana. That was probably one of the weirdest things (I have experienced in recruiting)."

Bennett also had another interesting experience in recruiting. It involved Alabama and then-coach Wimp Sanderson.

"Wimp Sanderson said he would have my name in lights up in a marquee outside of the arena," added Bennett.

In 1983, a few days after the well-publicized Dream Game in the NCAA tournament in Knoxville, the UK athletics board directed then-athletic director Cliff Hagan to come up with a deal to play a regular-season series with U of L. Both Hagan and coach Joe B. Hall opposed the opening of the series with a state school, especially Louisville, believing the popular Wildcats had nothing to gain and everything to lose.

Both schools eventually signed to play a regular-season series. And the series' first matchup was set for Nov. 26, 1983, marking the first regular-season game played between both schools since 1922. Interestingly, that was going to be Bennett's first game in a Wildcat uniform, facing against his hometown university at Rupp Arena on national television. The second-ranked Cats easily won the matchup, beating the No. 6 Cardinals, 65-44.

But Bennett nearly had to sit out the opener after spraining his ankle in practice a couple of days before. After hurting his ankle, he became very downhearted, thinking he would have to miss the game. The determined player, however, recovered in time to play a key role in the victory.

"We didn't think he would be able to play at all," Hall commented. The coach added that Bennett played super defense.

Although Bennett missed all of his six field goal tries and had four fouls in a reserve role, he grabbed seven rebounds and hit two free throws.

And the Wildcats continued to beat Louisville most of the time while Bennett attended UK. During his five years at Kentucky, including a redshirt season of 1986-87, Bennett and the Cats were 5-1 against U of L.

During the 32-4 season of 1985-86, Bennett, a junior, pumped in a then career-high 23 points in a 69-64 victory over Louisville. Bennett said that was his finest contest against the Cardinals. Afterwards, a disappointed coach Crum commented Bennett played his best game he had ever seen.

The UK-U of L series was a big deal for Bennett's parents. "It meant a lot to them," Bennett said. "It was bragging rights in the state of Kentucky when Kentucky and U of L played. For me I still lived in Louisville in the off-season and went back home on weekends (during the school year). My friends were all big U of L fans. It was (and is) always a tremendous rivalry for us."

Bennett played for two coaches at Kentucky. He had Hall for the first two years and the rest under then-coach Eddie Sutton.

Bennett had an outstanding freshman year as the Wildcats, led by twin towers — seniors Sam Bowie and Melvin Turpin, went to the 1984 Final Four in Seattle. He was a significant contributor to the team, making several All-SEC freshman teams and averaged 6.5 points and 3.8 rebounds.

He said going to the Final Four was his most memorable moment at Kentucky even though the Wildcats dropped to Georgetown in a 53-40 massacre. In the second half, Kentucky shot an horrendous 9.1 percent of its shots (3-for-33), finishing with a shooting percentage of less than 25 percent for the game.

During his sophomore year, foul-proned Bennett (along with junior Kenny Walker) was named co-captain of the team. The Wildcats, lacking experienced starters after the loss of Bowie, Turpin and Jim Master, struggled at the beginning of the season.

Plagued by pre-season difficulties involving Bennett, who had pneumonia and underwent knee surgery, and James Blackmon, Kentucky started with a rare 1-4 mark. It was the worst start UK has had since the 1920s.

Recovering from the surgery, Bennett wasn't able to play and missed several Blue-White scrimmages and the season opener with Toledo. It took him several games into the season before he finally took charge, finishing as the team's third-leading scorer in the 1984-85 campaign despite fouling out 10 times.

As it turned out, unranked Kentucky, with its 16-12 record, surprised everyone when it played well in the NCAA tournament, defeating Washington and Nevada-Las Vegas before losing to St. John's in the West Regional. The Cats completed with an 18-13 worksheet and Hall announced his retirement after the game with St. John's.

Then Sutton entered the Wildcat Country from Arkansas with impressive coaching credentials, including a NCAA Final Four appearance in 1978.

The "Hall to Sutton" changing of guard wasn't as difficult as some people had expected. The team adjusted well, Bennett said.

"There wasn't a tremendous difference," he explained. "Coach Hall had the advantage of having the Twin Towers, Bowie and Turpin. Everything ran through Bowie and Turpin. Eddie Sutton was more a big-guard type of coach. He liked his big guards like Rex Chapman and James Blackmon. He was really more open in his offense during that period of time. I thought the team really transferred that (coaching philosophy) tremendously well. It wasn't as difficult as you thought it would have been."

But Bennett refused to make comparisons between Hall and Sutton as far as their personalities were concerned. He didn't want to take sides. He obviously likes them both.

"Both guys were pretty easy going," Bennett said. "Both coaches had a lot of pressure on them to win. I don't like to put one coach against the other. They were both good coaches in their own right.

"Coach Hall came in and took over after a legend in

coach Adolph Rupp. It would have been difficult for any coach but coach Hall did an outstanding job."

During the Sutton regime, Bennett became more mature physically and twice earned All-SEC honors (1986 and '88). As a junior, Bennett scored 26 points, including hitting 14 of 16 free throws, against Tennessee at Rupp Arena as Kentucky triumphed 74-57.

In the mid-summer after the 1985-86 season, Bennett and his teammates got to experience some cultural shock in a trip to the Orient. They participated in a seven-game tour in Japan and Hong Kong, winning six games. It was Bennett's first trip overseas.

"The people looked up to the American players," Bennett recalled. "We had a lot of height and they usually don't. For the most part, they would walk up to you and measure themselves. It was a great trip for me."

Later, the defensive specialist had to sit out the 1986-87 campaign after undergoing a knee surgery as the result of an injury suffered in a pre-season practice. Bennett's absence was a severe blow to the young team, which had freshmen Rex Chapman, Reggie Hanson (who was ineligible due to Prop 48 academic standards) and Derrick Miller. The Wildcats sorely needed Bennett, who was a pre-season All-American candidate, for his senior leadership (along with Blackmon) after losing All-American Kenny Walker and playmaker Roger Harden.

It was a disturbing time for Bennett, who had looked forward to his senior year. He was very upset about the injury.

"(I was) extremely disappointed and frustrated," Bennett recalled. "I was in practice and we were running our pre-season drills. We had gotten in an up-and-down type of scrimmage. Ed Davender had come driving down the lane and shot the ball so I went up and rebounded and somebody fell into my knee."

Without Bennett, the Wildcats compiled an 18-11 mark as Chapman, a 6-4 guard, led the team with a 16.0-point average.

But, in the following season, a scrappy Bennett

recovered from his surgery and guided the sixth-ranked Cats to a remarkable 27-6 mark as a fifth-year senior. Later, UK's record was changed to 25-5 due to the NCAA sanctions in 1989, deleting Kentucky's three NCAA tournament games from official records.

It is nice to be a part of the UK basketball program, but it has some drawbacks. The players sometimes have too much exposure.

"They are living in a fishbowl," Bennett acknowledged. "Everybody is watching players. They have to be more than just regular humans. You don't hear that often about a regular human making a mistake, but at the university if a player makes the most minute mistake, the press and TV will tell about it.

"People put these players on pedestals but they are just normal people. They are still kids at this point. It is hard for them to realize just coming in here the magnitude of this program and how people project them. The procedure is something you have to learn once you get in the program but you get a lot of exposure."

Kentucky associate coach Jim O'Brien, who joined the Wildcats in 1994 after spending five years as the head coach at Dayton, agrees that the UK program is very big. For two years, O'Brien also had worked under Pitino on the New York Knicks coaching staff.

"I don't think anybody could realize how big it is at Kentucky," O'Brien told the author in *The Daily News* of Middlesboro. "You know, when we were with the New York Knicks, we thought it was big there — being in the Big Apple and all the hoopla that goes around there. But until you get affiliated with the University of Kentucky, you don't know what big-time basketball is all about."

Meanwhile, as an assistant coach, Bennett doesn't care for the NCAA rules. He thinks there are too many of them.

"These coaches have enough pressure on them as it is — bringing young people in, trying to hone them into men and see they go to classes," Bennett explained. "Rules about staying in a certain type of curricula under the NCAA are just too much. NCAA is trying to police college basketball. Some rules are trivial and are not doing a lot for the college game.

"These players have their own lives outside of college basketball. You try to look after them as much as possible, but you can't stay with them 24 hours a day."

Bennett's first coach in the NBA was Lenny Wilkens, whose Cleveland Cavaliers' club had selected the UK player in the third round of the 1988 NBA Draft. Bennett cherished his relationship with Wilkens, who is currently the NBA's winningest coach with the Atlanta Hawks.

"We had a tremendous relationship," said Bennett, who also briefly played pro basketball in Italy. "He is a very soft-spoken and respectful coach. He respects his players. You will never hear him curse at a player and very seldom see him get really upset. I really liked his style and you knew what he wanted out of you. He was low key."

And what did Wilkens think about Bennett? He once said he thought Bennett worked too hard.

While at Cleveland, Bennett did not make the All-NBA teams, but he had many good moments. He was a starter most of the time and played most of his three-year NBA career (1989-92) with the Cavaliers.

In a 1991 game against the visiting New Jersey Nets and center Sam Bowie, Bennett pumped in 23 points and hauled in 12 rebounds, helping Cleveland to an 108-82 victory. After the game, Bowie, who was Bennett's former teammate at UK, complimented Bennett, calling him a workaholic who does all the dirty work.

Bennett, who was known for his defensive prowess, said his best NBA game was in the 1990 post-season playoffs.

"We were playing Philadelphia and Charles Barkley in the playoffs," he said. "I had one of my best games against Charles. I had 22 points. I played defense on him and he played defense on me. I don't remember how many points he scored, but I was able to get 22 points. I was pretty excited about that."

But Cleveland, which finished with a regular season mark of 42-40, didn't advance in the playoffs, as it lost the opening round in five games. In the playoffs with the victorious 76ers, Bennett averaged 10 points.

His parents, who drove from Louisville, also saw him play in the northern Ohio city several times.

"They came to Cleveland on a number of occasions to see our home games," Bennett said. "It's a six-hour drive from Louisville to Cleveland."

And it was during that time when he decided to marry a young lady from his hometown whom he had known for many years.

"We grew up in the same church — Christ Temple Apostolic," Bennett said of his wife, Peggy. "We met each other at a very young age. It just evolved. We weren't childhood sweethearts. We started dating after college. We would talk back and forth on the phone when I was overseas. I played in Italy. We'd known each other all these times, merely friends. After I got back in the states, we kept in contact, got together on occasion.

"Once I signed the NBA contract, I found my life to be very lonely and I felt like I needed someone there so I called her one night and said, 'How would you like to get married,' and she said, 'Yes, let's do it.'

"So, the next couple of days after that, we were going to Atlanta around Christmas to play a game and I flew back to Louisville and married her (on December 23). I had to fly back out to play the Atlanta Hawks. We didn't see each other again until after the New Year."

Today, Bennett and his wife have two children, Leontay and Princess Victoria.

Bennett wished he had played longer in the NBA. His pro career was cut short with a serious knee injury in the off-season.

"My three years with Cleveland were tremendous years," Bennett commented. "NBA basketball was fantastic. It was a dream that I had worked on since I was eight to 10 years old. The Lord has allowed me to play those three years. I would have liked to play longer but it was a blessing to play those three (years) and I am very appreciative."

An Academic All-SEC pick in 1985, Bennett admitted that it was easier to play in the NBA. Unlike college, he didn't have to worry about the homework or studying for the exam.

"I'm sure it makes a difference that you can concentrate solely on basketball rather than academics and basketball," he said. "But I wouldn't trade those years I spent going to class and getting a good solid education for anything in the world."

In 1987, Bennett earned his bachelor's degree in business administration before his playing days ended at UK. "I started on MBA when I was here at Kentucky," he said, adding that one of his ambitions is to go back and complete a master's in business.

Bennett's short NBA career actually came to an end in the summer of 1992 when he worked out at a gym in Ohio where he was still living at the time. He had injured his knee. The ex-Wildcat, who had finished out the previous season with Miami after being released by Cleveland, was preparing for the Miami Heat pre-season camp.

"(I was) just running up and down the court and I felt a popping in the back of my knee," he said. "From then on my knee would swell real big and hurt and pain me. I thought ice treatments would take care of the swelling but it never did. When I went to the (training) camp in Miami; the knee just couldn't hold up. I couldn't bear the pain. I came back to Cleveland and had it checked out. They told me that I had torn my medial and lateral muscle in my knee. That ended my NBA career right there."

Bennett's faith is Apostolic. He says he depends on the Lord for everyday guidance. He is not ashamed to say that he is a Christian.

"It's everything that my life is based on," Bennett said of his religion. "As you go through life, sometimes you leave your faith or sometimes you stray from your faith and you find that's when problems happen. As your foundation, you always go back to it and see where you made your mistakes. My faith is key to me. It is simply believing in the Lord Jesus Christ and being baptized in Jesus' name and being filled with the Holy Ghost.

"That's what keeps me going everyday because I know that when problems arise I can go to Him in prayer, reading the Word and hopefully come out of it strong.

"The most interesting part is just believing in the Lord and putting my trust in Him. I don't think you can get more interesting than that. Don't stray from the belief in the Lord Jesus Christ because He says as long as you believe in Him you can do all things — it strengthens you.

Even when things are going well for you, you still need to give God the glory and the praise because He's the one who allows excellent things to happen.

"I hope to be a head coach someday. That's why I'm here. That's what this is about. This is not about me just being an assistant coach. This is a building block, the first step to becoming a head coach. To sit in a seat like coach Pitino is, not necessarily that one but somewhere. I would like to coach in the NBA."

12 Hoops Pioneer
BERNADETTE LOCKE-MATTOX

In the early summer of 1990, Bernadette Locke (now Locke-Mattox) — who was working as an assistant coach for the women's team at her alma mater, the University of Georgia — was pleasantly surprised when she received a phone call from coach Rick Pitino, one of the biggest names in basketball.

Pitino, who had just completed his first season at UK, informed Locke-Mattox that she was one of the people being considered for the asssistant coaching job on the men's team at Kentucky. Since they had never met each other before, he asked her to come to Lexington for an interview.

"He said he was looking to place his volunteer assistant with a female and wanted to know if I was interested," recalled Locke-Mattox, who knew of Pitino by watching him on TV when he guided Providence in the 1987 NCAA Final Four and the New York Knicks in the NBA. "It totally took me by surprise. Shocked? Yes. Elated. Getting the call from coach Pitino. I thought about it for a couple of days and called him back and said that I would come up for an interview after I consulted my fiancé (Vincent), who is my husband now."

Although Locke-Mattox had visited the UK campus many times before as a player and assistant coach for the

Georgia Lady Bulldogs, Pitino warned her in the interview that the men's basketball program at Kentucky was very big and that she would be under a lot of scrutiny from the fans and the media.

"You know how big Georgia football is?" Pitino asked her.

"Yeah," said Locke-Mattox.

"Well, multiply this about 10 times," said the Wildcat mentor.

"You're kidding?" said a surprised Locke-Mattox who opened her mouth in amazement.

On her interview, Locke-Mattox said she "felt good" afterwards but didn't know for sure if she had the job.

"I went back (home) and the coach was still inter-viewing a couple of other people," said Locke-Mattox, who had not gone through many job interviews at the time. "I thought it (the interview) went well. I had a good time and got to meet everybody at Kentucky. I really felt good about the people and I guess you just get an inner feeling of the atmosphere. I had a feeling that the guys were just a (part of the) family-oriented atmosphere.

"I had a few days to think about it prior to him call-ing me back and offering me the job. Even if I didn't get the job, I knew there were some good things going on at the University of Kentucky."

For Locke-Mattox, accepting her new job at Kentucky meant less pay, but it was an opportunity she couldn't refuse in becoming one of the first women to coach on a men's team in NCAA Division I.

"I had left a regular job to become a volunteer assistant and took a pay cut," she said.

Since UK didn't pay Locke-Mattox out of its uni-versity funds because of her post as a volunteer assistant, she was paid as a director of Pitino's summer basketball camps.

When the media learned of Pitino's plan to hire a woman assistant coach, some members cried foul. They claimed Pitino was creating a cheap publicity stunt for the program. But the UK coach, who acknowledged that this unusual coaching move would generate mostly-favorable public relations for the team, said the new coach would have the same duties as the other assistants.

Locke-Mattox, who has a bachelor's degree in education, said she didn't have any reservations about taking the men's job. Because of her background, she knew she'd be fairly comfortable in men's basketball. She also had friends on the men's team at Georgia.

"I had no second thoughts about it because I trusted him (Pitino)," Locke-Mattox commented. "Coach Pitino told me what my role would be and that I would be involved in the day-to-day activities of coaching and those types of things.

"Young people are young people and they haven't been around the college atmosphere as long as I have. They just want to know that they're loved, that they're cared for and the things that they're being taught are right, if you're indeed a coach. So, for that part, I had no skepticism at all."

An editorial in UK's student daily newspaper, *Kentucky Kernel*, questioned Pitino's hiring of Locke-Mattox. It said the hiring was apparently based on the applicant's sex, not qualifications. While Pitino's actions on opening a door of opportunities for women are commendable, the best qualified person should be one chosen for the position, said the student newspaper.

Locke-Mattox, a native of Philadelphia, Tennessee, doesn't really consider herself a pioneer in women's movement, especially in the coaching profession. But she is pleased to know that her well-publicized move to the men's program may open some doors for women coaches who are struggling for respect and equal opportunities.

"I feel good that I, as a woman, had the opportunity to maybe instill in other women that they have the ability or the capability nowadays to do whatever they want to do. Whether it's getting into the men's side of basketball or becoming an astronaut or whatever it is that they want to do. (It might) help them to say, 'Hey, yes, I can do that.' Women can do whatever they want to do."

There have been other women who were involved with the men's program. For instance, at Georgetown University, Mary Fenlon served as an assistant on coach John Thompson's staff, but she primarily worked on the academic side.

But Locke-Mattox is considered the country's first bona-fide woman assistant coach on a prestigious men's team. Because of her status, she received a lot of national coverage, including *People's Weekly, New York Times*, and network TV interviews, among others. She could've had a lot more press coverage had not she turned down the interview requests. The interviews had taken too much of her time away from coaching.

Pitino didn't really warn her that she would get a lot of press because of her position, according to Locke-Mattox, who ended up coaching the men's team for four years before becoming an assistant athletic director at UK (for one year) and later the head coach of the UK women's basketball program. The coach just told her, in general terms, that the men's program has a big following.

"The only thing he said was to understand that the press will be involved just because Kentucky is a high-profile team," she said. "I knew that because I knew the excitement of Kentucky and their tradition. It's bigger than I would have ever thought.

"I've got to credit Chris Cameron (ex-UK sports information director), who really kept the press away from me so I could do my job, which was coaching. On the bigger things that were necessary, I was there for the interviews. But on the day-to-day badgering and interviewing, he really kept that away from me and I've got to appreciate Chris Cameron and coach (Pitino) for that. I came here to do a job and that allowed me to do my job. So there wasn't a lot of press. There could have been a lot more — it could've been crazy."

Locke-Mattox said her most interesting interview occurred a few years ago when a group of aspiring journalists from a Kentucky high school did a 30-minute television show with her.

"That's the one which really stands out," said Locke-Mattox. "I wish I could remember the school (that did the interview). It was in Kentucky. They came in, set it up, did the microphones and did the lighting. They asked the best questions. It was fun. Those kids were so excited about being there and having the opportunity to interview me and say, 'This was my project.' They wanted everything to be right, every question to be right. And it was good. I think they showed it in their hometown (on local cable TV) and I hope it went well for them."

Like most new jobs, her first few months at UK weren't a breeze. Locke-Mattox, who also helped the players with career placement and academics in addition to coaching, had to adjust to her new surroundings at work and home. And, as a Wildcat assistant, she remembers her first practice.

"Everybody was huge," she said. "I kind of felt pint-sized. Other than having to look up to the players all the time and to be careful about not getting in the way a lot, it was okay. I felt confident in myself and the things that coach (Pitino) expected me to do.

"I think any coach, whether it's a male or female, going into a new job, it's going to take awhile for the players (to accept). Once the players understand that you care about them, you love them, you're there for them and you know what you're talking about, you're okay."

One of her Wildcat players, forward John Pelphrey, admired Locke-Mattox. "She is the mother of 15 guys, who she not only pushes to the limit on the floor, but in the classroom as well," stated Pelphrey in 1991. "And she is without question the most beautiful All-American of all time."

Another Kentucky player, guard Travis Ford, later commented that she had been a positive influence, adding that she would make a good head coach someday.

Outside of coaching, she also had another adjustment. Vincent Mattox, her future husband, whom she met in Athens, Georgia, in the early 1980s, wasn't around. They had been engaged for several months after dating for about five years.

A former University of Virginia football player, Vincent stayed in Georgia, working as a teacher and coach at Athens Academy, a private school. He coached football, girls' basketball and track. "I guess you kind of wear a lot of hats at a small, private school," said Locke-Mattox of her husband's coaching duties.

Because of their careers, she and Vincent had to develop a long-distance relationship.

"We did it for two years," Locke-Mattox commented. "I wanted to get my feet planted here and he had a career there. (Before he would) uproot and come up here quickly, especially when I was a volunteer, he really wanted to be sure this coaching position was what I wanted to do and to be sure that it was a good situation. So it was tough. I think any long-distance relationship is tough. We love each other totally. We got married the second year that I was here (at Kentucky)."

Did her future husband encourage her to accept the Kentucky job?

"Oh, yes," said Locke-Mattox. "He was totally supportive of it and I couldn't thank him enough for his support. He's the kind of man who will always support me and be there. He's just been wonderful. I couldn't ask for a better person to be married to and to be my soulmate."

Vincent eventually gave up his job at Athens Academy to be with his wife in Lexington. He took a state government position with the Kentucky Department of Education in Frankfort as a consultant.

The couple have one son, who interestingly was

born on Mother's Day in 1995. A proud Locke-Mattox said it was the best gift a mom could possibly have.

Locke-Mattox said her most difficult moment as a Wildcat assistant came in March 1992. Kentucky had lost to top-ranked and eventual national champion Duke in a 104-103 overtime thriller in what many observers described as one of the greatest, if not the greatest, NCAA tournament games ever played.

Needless to say, she and her husband were very downhearted after the NCAA East Regional championship game. They just sat in the hotel room at Philadelphia.

"That was tough," Locke-Mattox said of the setback. "It was tough because of the heart that the players gave. They gave their all in that game and to feel what they felt on top of what you felt, it was tough. That was probably the toughest thing that I've had to deal with besides the death of my father."

The Wildcats, who were making their first trip to the NCAA tournament since 1988, had bounced back from a 12-point deficit in the second half before taking the matchup to overtime. With UK down by one point, senior playmaker Sean Woods pumped in a potential game-winning field goal with 2.1 seconds remaining in the game. But national player-of-the-year Christian Laettner stunned everyone when he poured in a buzzer-beating basket to give Duke a victory.

A transfer from Roane State Community College in Harriman, Tennessee, Locke-Mattox played two years of basketball at Georgia, earning All-American honors after her junior year (1979-80).

She also captured All-SEC honors twice and led the league with an average of over four steals a game in 1979-80. In her senior year, she led the Lady Bulldogs (27-10) to the 1981 National Women's Invitational Tournament crown.

After receving her degree, she didn't go anywhere. She remained at the school, serving as a graduate assistant coach for the women's team for two years under the guidance of Andy Landers, who is now one of the winningest active NCAA Division I coaches in women's basketball.

By the way, it was Landers who brought Locke-Mattox with him to Georgia when he became the head coach in 1979. He was also her coach at Roane State Community College.

With her education degree, Locke-Mattox could've already begun her teaching career at an elementary school and forgotten about basketball. Originally, teaching was her plan.

"I wanted to teach school and didn't even think about coaching," she said. "I wanted to be a teacher. I wanted to teach the little kids. That was a passion of mine."

In 1984, Locke-Mattox left Georgia to try out a new profession outside athletics — the business world. She attended the DeVry Institute of Technology in Atlanta, studying computer science, and worked for the Xerox corporation.

Things, however, didn't really work out and she went back to Athens in 1985 to coach. She became an assistant coach and recruiting coordinator for the Lady Bulldogs. During her five-year tenure as an assistant coach at Georgia, the powerful Lady Bulldogs posted a composite mark of 126-29, including five trips to the NCAA tournament.

When Locke-Mattox played basketball in college, she wore knee-high socks. That was the style back in late 1970s and early 1980s. And about 10 years later, those socks would make a return appearance at a Wildcat practice session, embarrassing assistant coach Locke-Mattox.

"One day I came out to practice, and all the players, the coach and the staff had their socks pulled up to their knees," recalled Locke-Mattox. "That was the most embarrassing thing. They said, 'This is way back, coach Locke. We're now pretending to be you with our socks pulled up.' So they always gave me a hard time about it. They always called me 'High Socks.'

"There was a picture of me, I think, in one of the women's old press guides (at Georgia). Somehow they'd got this picture. I don't know if they called the sports information people at Georgia, but they got this full-blown picture of me with my socks all the way up. They had blown it up and hung it up. I was embarrassed to see the picture. God, that was years ago."

She said this incident turns out to be her most embarrassing moment as an assistant coach at UK.

Besides coaching, one of Locke-Mattox's career goals was sports administration. She wanted to become an athletic director some day. It wouldn't be easy though as less than 15 percent of the university administrators in the athletic department are female, according to recent figures. In the spring of 1993, she turned down an offer from Pitino to move from part-time assistant to full-time assistant and a nice increase in pay. She was still waiting for her turn to work in the administration.

Her turn came after the 1993-94 campaign. She quit coaching to accept a position in UK's athletic department. As the school's first black high-ranking sports administrator, she supervised eight non-revenue sports, monitored athletic department compliance with Title IX and gender equity guidelines, and managed all events held in Memorial Coliseum. Working for athletic director C. M. Newton made her decision to change jobs easier.

"It was a great opportunity for me to work under a great person like C. M. (Newton)," Locke-Mattox said. "He's just so knowledgeable and so respected around the country. Becoming an athletic director was one of my ultimate goals. I couldn't have picked a better person than he (Newton) and Larry Ivy (senior associate athletic director) to learn from.

"I was at a point in my life and my career where I needed a change. Not to say that I was tired of coaching. No, I enjoyed it. But I was at a point in my life where family outweighed a lot of different things. I wanted to have children."

But Locke-Mattox, now in late 30s, didn't stay on the new job very long — about 10 months. Even being pregnant, she couldn't resist an opportunity to coach again. In March of 1995, she was named the head coach of the women's team at UK, replacing Sharon Fanning, whose contract wasn't renewed. (Fanning later took a similar job at Mississippi State.)

Two months later, UK announced that the women's basketball team would no longer be called the Lady Kats. Locke-Mattox had requested the change and wanted her new team to be referred to as the Wildcats.

Before taking over the women's hoops program, Locke-Mattox admitted that she did miss coaching while working as an assistant athletic director and hadn't ruled out a return to the hardwood floor some day. She said, "I'm going to keep that chapter open in my book in the event that I have to go back or want to go back. I miss it."

Her former boss, Rick Pitino, was pleased that she took the coaching post. "I believe she will be the premier recruiter in women's basketball," said Pitino, who has compiled a six-year UK record of 150-43 going into the winter of 1995-96. "I look forward to the day when both of our programs will be ranked No. 1."

Locke-Mattox has been a participant on both sides — as a player or coach for women's teams at Georgia and UK, and men's assistant coach at Kentucky. She recognizes that women's college basketball is still struggling as far as attendance and media attention are concerned despite some improvements. That's unfortunate, she said.

"I feel bad because I know the women give their sweat and heart just like the men do, but I understand TV and I understand media," Locke-Mattox commented. "I understand that because I've been in both places. To say it's fair, no, but I understand what the advertisers and sponsors want.

"It's just unfortunate that they're not supported media-wise as the men. We, as a university, can't control what the media, the sponsors, people want. We would love for them (women) to be on TV every night. We would love for them to have that type of backing. That type of bodies in the seats, but unfortunately, the administration and the coaches can't do it."

What about the men's hoops program? Do they get too much fanfare? Yes, perhaps, but the Wildcats, for the most part, enjoy the adulation or the media exposure which comes with the territory of being a part of the tradition-rich program.

"They can't be like a regular student," she said of the players. "I can feel for them playing in such a fishbowl. They can't go out without being hounded by the fans. But because Kentucky is what it is, they have to deal with that. Not to say that it's bad or good, but sometimes it does get to be a little too much with the public because you can't go anywhere and relax or eat a meal without that (scrutiny).

"Sometimes it gets hectic. They're trying to study. They're trying to be like the regular student. It does gets a little crazy when you're always having to go to the media. When they have to run from a class, go to the media and then go to practice, it does get a little crazy. You know they want maybe some time to relax for a minute before they go to practice.

"The young people want to get to them — the little kids. Our players don't mind that. There's a price that you've got to pay for being at UK. But for the most part, it's fun (for the players). It's enjoyable."

Kentucky has always been under a heavy spotlight. It's inevitable that the Wildcats will be criticized every now and then. When the fans and the media get upset about a controversial move or losing, Pitino and his coaching staff don't tell the players what to say, according to Locke-Mattox.

"He tries to help them to understand why there are negatives around," said Locke-Mattox. "You've got to understand that you're not always going to be liked. There are always going to be negative things said, but understand why that happens and then try not to feel bad. I think if you can understand why those things are happening, you can deal with them better."

And on the players' interviews with the media, "Coach (Pitino) wants them to answer as honestly as possible," said Locke-Mattox. "I think he will never tell our guys what to say. We want them to be positive and upbeat. But, you know, they've got to say what they feel. So the coach and the staff will never tell the guys what to say because he wants them to be honest and be truthful to the questions. You always want them to be positive to everything around them."

As a teenager, Locke-Mattox did not play a conventional basketball game of five players on each team in Tennessee. While at Loudon County High School, a class AA member, near her small rural hometown of

Philadelphia, she played three-on-three games.

Locke-Mattox was an outstanding prep player. She didn't consider herself the star of the squad, which went to the state finals her senior year before losing.

"We had seven girls on our basketball team who were seniors and we all played as freshmen coming up," she said. "A star? No. We were all really good — kind of equal. We had different roles. I didn't see myself as a star. It wasn't perceived that way or talked up that way when I was coming up. We are still friends now and we stay in touch and we get together every once in a while. So the friendship that we gathered at that young age is still there."

Playing basketball, however, wasn't very high on her list of activities while growing up.

"I wasn't interested in basketball until my later years when I started playing in the seventh grade," Locke-Mattox commented. "(Basketball) wasn't one of my goals when I was younger. I mean there were so many things going on around us."

Even before she began playing basketball in the early 1970s, Locke-Mattox got interested in the sport when she saw ex-NBA star Walt Frazier of the New York Knicks play on television.

"I kind of got interested in the game by watching him play," she said. "I wasn't a big basketball person at all. Walt Frazier was a point guard and I really enjoyed the way he played, his style of play. I never would see him fight. If anybody pushed him or anything like that, he'd just go down to the other end and score on them. He didn't hurt them physically, but he hurt them where it really hurt — in points."

While Knoxville is only about a one-hour drive from her home in Philadelphia, Locke-Mattox wasn't interested in the new Lady Vols program, which had begun in 1974. By the time Locke-Mattox graduated from high school in 1977, coach Pat Head (now Pat Summitt) had guided Tennessee to a 28-5 record in her third year of coaching.

"I was never interested," Locke-Mattox said of the Lady Vols, who recruited her out of high school. "I chose not to attend the University of Tennessee."

So Locke-Mattox decided to attend a local junior college. "The reason I chose Roane State was because we played three-on-three when I was in high school," she explained. "It wasn't five-on-five. I wanted to get better at five-on-five. I felt, at that time, it was better for me to go to Roane State under Andy Landers to learn how to play five-on-five rather than to sit on the bench somewhere else and not learn how to play. Even though I was a good player, I felt it would be a great opportunity for me to learn and, at the same time, play."

As it turned out, it was a good move on her part.

What kind of person is Locke-Mattox, a very attractive lady who once aspired to be a model? Despite her celebrity status, she would like the people to know her as a friendly person.

"I'm down to earth," said the Tennessee native, a Presbyterian, who loves reading autobiographies and novels in the summer when she has the time. "I'm always going to be Bernadette. I'm not going to deviate from that. I'm not going to change. And I think I've grown as an individual as you do from so many different jobs and so many different areas. I'll always stop every chance I get and get a reality check because I'm no better than anybody and I don't want anybody to feel any better than I am. God put us all here to live together and work together and I want to eat and dine with anybody I feel like."

13 Chief Cat
C.M. NEWTON

As the newly-hired athletic director at Kentucky, C. M. Newton's first major move came in the late spring of 1989 when he grabbed charismatic coach Rick Pitino away from the bright lights of New York City. The highly-publicized hiring came a few days after the *Sports Illustrated* magazine ran a cover story ("Kentucky's Shame") in its May 29 edition about Kentucky's scandal and near-death penalty sanctions imposed by the NCAA.

After Pitino had turned down Newton's initial offer several weeks earlier, Newton admitted that he was somewhat surprised that he had finally lured Pitino away from the NBA. The boyish-looking mentor had just guided the New York Knicks to a 52-30 record with a first-place finish in the Atlantic Division. The Wildcats actually lucked out to get him, said the athletic director.

"I was (surprised), particularly based on the early conversations we had," Newton said from his office at UK's Memorial Coliseum. "I knew he had an interest in coming to college, but the nature of the timing and with the Knicks (in the playoffs) and Rick's loyalty to them (almost made it impossible for him to leave New York). I use the word luck. We were lucky there in that they (the Knicks management) kind of screwed it up. They kind of gave us an opening.

"Once he came and visited (Lexington), I was not surprised. At that point, I would have bet the house that he was going to be our coach."

Had UK not landed Pitino, would Newton himself agree to coach the Wildcats for one year until a suitable replacement could be found?

"No, what I said was, at the time, I wasn't going to be pressured either by public opinion or media attention or what other people thought if we couldn't get the right coach," Newton said. "And somebody asked me, 'Well, what would you do? Here you are almost into June.' And I said, 'Hell, if I have to, I'll coach them myself.' "

Newton commented that it would've been bad for the school's athletic program if he had to coach. Wearing two hats as the athletic director and basketball coach would've been overwhelming for one person, especially in today's environment.

"That would have been the worst scenario for me," stated Newton. "(The dual position is) too much for anybody. It would have been bad for me and bad for the team."

But the former coach acknowledged that it might've been "a better option than getting the wrong guy."

In Nashville, during the 1988-89 campaign, a lot of rumors floated around about Newton, who was coaching at Vanderbilt. The media speculated that he had agreed in principle to become UK's athletic director, replacing Cliff Hagan, who was forced by the university administration to resign in the wake of a growing scandal. UK attorney Joseph Burch, meanwhile, served as the school's acting athletic director in the interim.

When his Vanderbilt squad came to Lexington in

early January to face the embattled coach Eddie Sutton and the Wildcats, Newton didn't want to discuss the situation. He didn't confirm or deny his strong interest in the UK job.

About two weeks later, Newton entered a new chapter of his athletic career. He officially accepted the AD post at Kentucky, his alma mater. He would start to work at his new job after finishing the season with the Commodores.

But Newton's decision in the middle of the season drew criticism. His players, as well as the Commodore fans, were angry and dumfounded. But not all of them. Some understood the awkward situation as Newton said he didn't want to mislead or lie to folks that he wasn't interested in the Kentucky job. He even received a standing ovation in the pre-game introduction of the Vandy-Florida matchup in Nashville the day after he took the Kentucky post.

Dr. David Roselle, then president at UK, called Newton's hiring "a new day for Kentucky athletics." Roselle hired Newton — a down-to-earth gentleman well known for his integrity and his loyalty for UK — since the school's basketball program, being investigated by the NCAA, had started to fall apart.

But Newton — who played on UK's 1951 national championship squad for legendary coach Adolph Rupp — almost didn't come to Kentucky. He and his wife, Evelyn, loved Vanderbilt and the Music City. It actually took more than a couple of months before Newton finally said okay.

Shortly, after Cliff Hagan resigned his AD position on Nov. 15, Roselle placed a call to Newton, asking if he would be interested in coming to UK.

"I told him at the time I had absolutely no interest in doing it," said Newton, who was preparing the Commodores for the upcoming season. "I had some anger and frustration. Cliff was a very good friend of mine. He was a teammate of mine and I thought he'd done a good job here. It bothered me that he was pushed into a forced resignation.

"I was not very receptive then. I told Dr. Roselle that. I really had no interest. I was coaching my team. I didn't want to be an athletic director."

But Roselle still wanted Newton, telling the Vandy coach, "Well, at some time, I'd like to have a chance to talk to you about our program and some of the things we need."

"Well, I might do that," Newton obliged.

Later, they ran into each other, and agreed to schedule a face-to-face meeting at UK's Elizabethtown Community College to discuss the situation at Kentucky. They met for three hours. The coach didn't make any decision, but drove home to Nashville on I-65 feeling good about Roselle.

"It was strictly information," Newton said of the meeting at Elizabethtown. "I had known through some of the others that I was kind of wanted (at Kentucky) but he convinced me that some of the things that I could bring to the table were needed. When your university — that you care about — put it that way, that's a pretty strong (message).

"So I went back home and I told Evelyn that I was very impressed with Dr. Roselle. I said, 'Evelyn, it seemed like that maybe right now there's a lot of division, at least in his mind, and maybe I'm needed. I'm going to really look at it.' I prayed about it and did all the things that you would want to do and made the decision that yes, I was going to do it."

Although they had moved a few times before, leaving Vanderbilt was very troublesome for the Newton family. They had a nice home and many friends in Nashville.

"Yes, that's the hardest place we've left," said Newton of his career. "It was very difficult for both of us to leave Vanderbilt for a lot of reasons. One, my age. When I left the conference office (in 1981 where Newton had been an assistant commissioner at SEC), I was in my early fifties. And I pretty much committed to her and to myself that (Vandy job) would probably be our last move. I was going to coach until they told me I couldn't coach any longer. I would like to have been able to plan to coach until life said, 'You're too old. You can't do it any longer.'

"And I never wanted to be an athletic director. I never really had any thought in mind about coming back to Lexington. It was a hard move, particularly hard for Evelyn. It's a move I'm really glad we made, but it was not an easy decision."

Newton, however, didn't always feel he had made the right career decision after taking the AD post. He sometimes had regrets. He still loved coaching and, while the NCAA investigation lingered on, he had many difficult administrative decisions to make.

"There were times during the early parts of it that I wondered what the heck I was doing here," Newton recalled. "There was such tension around the hiring of the coach and here I'm trying to figure into a new job and a new situation, knowing that one decision was probably going to be the most important one I'll make.

"If we get the right guy, we can bring everybody together and get on about our business. But if we get the wrong guy, we're going to go the way of UCLA — go through coach after coach after coach. I just didn't want that to happen to this program. Luckily, we were able to get Rick to come.

"During that time, I really missed coaching. I missed the contact with the athletes."

After 12 years of coaching at Transylvania College (now Transylvania University) in Lexington, a fairly young Newton moved on to bigger things in 1968, taking a job with the University of Alabama as the school's head basketball coach. Hired by the Crimson Tide athletic director and head football coach Paul "Bear" Bryant, Newton came to Alabama at a time when the southern schools struggled with the civil rights movement. The 1960s was a time of civil unrest, especially in the deep

South. The "Whites Only" signs were evident in many places.

"We were not that far removed from the real racial tensions that pervaded the entire South and the entire country," said Newton, who had already known Bryant when the Bear served as the head football coach at UK in the late 1940s and early 1950s.

Five years earlier, Alabama had made national headlines when Gov. George Wallace stood on the Tuscaloosa campus in an attempt to bar two black students from registering for classes. The students eventually enrolled after Wallace, who was a segregationist, had left the school.

And at the time of Newton's hiring at Alabama, the SEC had broken the racial barrier in basketball two years before. When Newton interviewed for the Alabama post, he asked Bryant about recruiting blacks for the squad. They agreed it was time to integrate the program. (Bryant, meanwhile, didn't have any black players on his football team at the time, but he eventually saw his first black players, John Mitchell—a junior college transfer— and Wilbur Jackson, play for the Crimson Tide in 1971.)

"He said just get the right kind of people," Newton recalled.

Newton already had been impressed with the basketball talent he discovered in the state of Alabama a few years earlier when he spent one season at Alabama, working on his doctorate.

"I had gone to some high school games," Newton explained. "The high school basketball in Alabama was segregated at the time. I went to the black state tournament and the talent level was unbelievable. In the white state tournament, it was just so-so and most of those guys, though, were going to Kansas, Michigan State and so on."

Newton didn't waste much time when he signed a black standout from Birmingham (Ala.) powerhouse Parker High by the name of Wendell Hudson in 1969, beating Bryant by a couple of years in signing a black player to a scholarship. And the 6-5 Hudson, who was generally overlooked on a star-studded prep squad which won the state championship, became the first black scholarshipped athlete in school history. Curiously, Alabama was the only major college which offered him a scholarship.

"The interesting thing about Wendell Hudson was that he was a good high school player, but was not one of the highly-recognized high school players," Newton said. "Actually we were recruiting another player on his team and that kid was also a great baseball player. And the question was whether he was going to go baseball or basketball. Well, he ended up being drafted by the Cleveland Indians. But every time I went to see him play, I couldn't get my eyes off Wendell. He did things so effortlessly. He was a great jumper."

Newton got to know Hudson. "(He) was just such a unique man," he said. "We were lucky. I mean it was a stroke of luck. When we decided to sign him, I think it scared me (since only a few schools had shown some interest in the player).

"I asked him who was recruiting him. The only people recruiting him were a couple of junior colleges and another college. Auburn had told him he wasn't strong enough to play in the SEC.

"But I finally decided that he could play and it didn't matter what other people thought. He wasn't out on any recruiting list. That didn't bother me. So all he did was come in there and he became the (SEC) Player of the Year for two years."

However, after signing a black player, Newton wasn't a very popular coach. To make matters worse, he had just completed his first season at the Crimson Tide helm with a sorry 4-20 record, including 1-17 in the SEC. (He improved in the second year, but still bad with an 8-18 record overall, including 5-13 in SEC.)

"It was controversial," Newton recalled. "He (Hudson) and I developed a very close relationship during that time because I got a lot of heat, too. We weren't winning and we'd signed the first black in any sport, so that doesn't endear you to the populace."

Despite the racial tensions on the campus, Hudson handled the situation real well. Newton obviously was proud of Hudson's efforts to get along with everybody.

"It was hard on him," Newton stated. "It was not just hard on the road. It was hard on him right in Alabama. It was hard on him in Bryant Hall (dormitory). There were some guys who didn't want us to bring black guys to Alabama. It was a very difficult situation for Wendell.

"The reason I say we were lucky was because he was the perfect person for that. He had a way about him of not being, you know, some namby-pamby guy. He had maturity and a wiseness about that whole business of relationships. It was unbelievable to see him (to handle the circumstances well)."

Hudson's arrival at Alabama opened the doors for other blacks. Newton began to get some outstanding players such as Ray Odums, Charles Cleveland, Leon Douglas and T. R. Dunn in the early 1970s as the downtrodden Crimson Tide began to improve, winning more often. "Wendell was the key," Newton said. "Had it not been for Wendell, we wouldn't have gotten Ray Odums." The 6-2 Odums came to Alabama in 1970 and eventually earned All-SEC honors three times at guard.

Newton's first winning season at Alabama came in his fourth year (1971-72) as the Crimson Tide posted an 18-8 mark with 13-5 in SEC play. A couple of years later, Alabama began its three-year string of SEC basketball titles (1974, '75 and '76) and became a perennial SEC power.

"We proved that you could win with local talent and that local talent just happened to be black," Newton said. "The thing that I'm most proud of at Alabama is that we took and destroyed the myth that you got a 'football state,' and that you couldn't compete nationally with your home-grown talent.

"We also destroyed some myths about the African-American or black youngster not being able to be in a disciplined environment. We destroyed myths about not being able to graduate. I'm very proud of the fact that in the 12 years I was there, we had only four guys who couldn't earn a degree. We built a program and we sustained it. And we did it in the right way."

Bryant once commented, "C. M. Newton is a winner, and that's important, but more than anything else he wins or loses with class, and that's more important."

University of Louisville color commentator Jock Sutherland is one of Newton's close friends. They even coached together at Alabama for a couple of seasons (1968 to '70) when Sutherland served as a Crimson Tide assistant. "We lost a whole lot," said Sutherland in 1995. "That wasn't easy, but I remember how strong C. M. was. I was breaking down, but he stayed with it."

After Hudson's playing days at Alabama ended, Newton asked the player to stay on. Hudson, an All-American forward in 1973, served as an assistant coach on Newton's staff. He remained there for six years.

According to Newton, Hudson should've gotten more recognition that he really deserves because of "his contribution to that program and it saddens me that he hasn't received the recognition.

"One of the regrets that I'll take with me to my grave was that I wouldn't hire Wendell when I went to Vandy (in 1981). He wanted to come with us and I should have hired Wendell. He was good. He was very special. But it was not an easy time."

At Vanderbilt, when Newton later returned to coaching after spending one year in the SEC office, he had one of his former aides at Alabama, John Bostick, on his Commodore staff but not Hudson.

At this writing, Hudson was coaching a women's junior college team in Waco, Texas, according to Newton.

He had previously coached at Baylor. "He decided he just didn't want to be on the road all the time," Newton said.

The duo still keep in touch as they share a special friendship.

Paul Bryant — who later became the winningest coach in major college football history — had been coaching the Crimson Tide for 10 years when Newton arrived at Alabama to coach basketball. The Bear had revived the school's once-proud football program to new heights, earning nine straight post-season bowl bids, including three national championships, during that 10-year span from 1958 to '67.

Alabama, whose fans treated Bryant as if he were a grand king, had become known as a football factory, one of the best, if not the best, in the country.

Did it bother Newton, being from the basketball-crazy state of Kentucky, that Alabama had a big football following? He was going to coach a sport that no local people cared about.

"I knew what I was getting into," he said. "All I wanted was to get basketball through that hurdle and I worked very hard to do that. I think you've got the reverse of that here (at Kentucky) and Bill (Curry) is experiencing that here.

"I have never felt that you can't have great football and basketball (programs) because when I was a student (at UK) we won two national championships and our football team went to the Orange, Sugar and Cotton bowls when there were only four (major) bowls. They didn't have all the bowls that you've got now.

"So anybody who has ever tried to tell me, 'Well, you know it's a basketball school or it's a football school,' I'll never believe that. I believe that if you truly work together, and you help each other and support each other, you can have great boths. And that's what we did at Alabama. For a period in the decade of the '70s, we were winning (three) national championships in football and we were competing for national championship in basketball. We never did win one, but we were highly-ranked as third in the nation. We had six years where we won 22 or more games. It was an exciting time."

While at Alabama, Newton faced his mentor, Adolph Rupp, on the hardwood floor eight times. Kentucky was the victor every time, but once.

On Feb. 28, 1972, Newton, then 42, won his first game against Rupp when the Crimson Tide defeated the Wildcats 73-70 in Tuscaloosa in Rupp's last year of coaching. The victory earned Newton the distinction of becoming the first and only former Rupp player to beat the Baron while he was a head coach.

After the game, both coaches walked toward each other and had their customary handshakes.

"Congratulations," Rupp said. "It was a tremendous win for you."

At that moment, Newton was on cloud nine, thinking, "Boy, finally, I'm a peer! I'm a coaching peer!"

But Rupp wasn't finished talking.

"But, Newton, you're trying to do too much offense. You've got to simplify some of the things you're trying."

"Well, coach, maybe we are. I don't know," commented the Alabama coach, who had now gone from being a peer back to being one of Rupp's boys again in a matter of seconds.

Newton later admitted that Rupp was right. "When I went back and looked (at the films), in all seriousness we were trying to do a little bit too much offense," he said.

On coaching against Rupp, Newton said, "I wanted

him to look at me not as one of his boys, but to look at me as a basketball coach, as a competitor and more of a peer. And I thought we'd kind of gotten to that level when I went to Alabama and coached against him. We had a couple of close games. But the night we won the game (against UK), our players were very excited because Kentucky didn't lose much then. They had a good team, but we were able to win the game. But he always said you're one of his boys."

Newton — who for many years had an assistant by the name of Wimp Sanderson who later became a highly successful Crimson Tide head coach — had several good moments at Alabama.

Besides wining three consecutive SEC championships in the mid-1970s, compiling a 67-14 (.827) mark over a three-year period, he guided the Crimson Tide to their first-ever NCAA tournament berth in 1975. Alabama lost in the tourney's first round, dropping to Arizona State 97-94 on the Sun Devils' home floor in Tempe, Arizona.

The following season saw the sixth-ranked Crimson Tide go all the way to the final 16 in the 1976 NCAA tournament. In the first tourney game, All-American center Leon Douglas led Alabama to a 79-64 victory over North Carolina with game-highs 35 points and 17 rebounds. Then the Crimsom Tide lost by five points to eventual national champion Indiana, which had standouts Kent Benson, Scott May and Quinn Buckner on its 32-0 squad.

"I think the one I will probably remember the most was a loss," said Newton, who was selected SEC Coach of the Year four times at Alabama. "The Indiana loss in 1976 was probably a highlight and a lowlight at the same time. It was a highlight in that our team probably played about as good as they could play in a classic game. That's the only team I ever had that I felt could be good enough to win a national championship. I knew that team was good enough. They peaked at the right time.

"We had destroyed a really good North Carolina team. We were at the top of our game and we played an Indiana team which ended up going undefeated. As far as a team, Indiana was the best team I ever saw. That and the (UK) Fabulous Five. But, to be that close, and to know if you get past that one, you can win it all. I'll always remember that because we would go down to the last shot in the last 15 seconds with the ball; we could've won it but didn't. Our team played as good as it could play."

By the way, these tournament matchups with North Carolina and Indiana were the first nationally-televised games Alabama ever had. The NBC network carried the games.

Both Newton and Indiana's Bobby Knight coached together on the U.S. basketball squad in the 1984 Olympics when the former served as team manager, which was a combination of coaching and administrative duties, under head coach Knight. They helped the U.S. to capture the gold medal. Knight may be one of the most controversial coaches around, but he is honest, according to Newton.

"He's one of my best friends," he said. "We have been very close for a long time. One of the things I admire about Bob is his honesty. He is one of the few totally honest people I know."

Knight likes to call the UK athletic director "the finest gentleman in our business."

But don't get the wrong idea that Newton approves of everything Knight has done.

"There are a lot of things that Bob does that I

wouldn't do, but there are also a lot of things that he does that I admire very much," Newton said.

In a separate interview with the author in 1984, Newton had this to say about Knight. "I think the difference (between us) is in approach. Bob is a little bit more shortfused, temper-wise than I am, although mostly whatever Bobby does, he is in complete control. But he fusses with the media. I would rather avoid that confrontation. He's more of a hollerer at practice than perhaps I am, but you know each person coaches to his own personality or I think he should."

Knight is known for his controversial comments as well as for being involved in several unforgettable incidents such as putting an LSU fan in a garbage can, throwing a chair on the floor, his altercation with a Puerto Rican policeman during the 1979 Pan American Games, badmouthing an NCAA official who mistakenly commented that Knight would not attend the post-game press conference during the 1995 NCAA tourney (his emotional outburst cost Indiana a $30,000 fine levied by the NCAA), to name a few. For such actions, he has received bad press.

"I think now he kind of likes the reputation and the rapport or the lack of rapport that he has with the media," Newton said. "He gets along very well with the people in the media that he respects. There are a lot of those guys he doesn't respect. Some of the media may not respect him. He just doesn't care to spend time with them.

"But it's unfortunate because what has happened is that the perception of him generated by the media for the most part has really overshadowed the greatness of his career and what he's done. The crazy things are what people think of with him. When you think of Bob Knight, you don't think of a guy who has spent most of his life in college, coaching and dedicating himself to fund-raising for the library at Indiana University.

"You don't see the tremendous bond, loyalty and love that he has (for his players) and that his players have for him. He's a unique guy. But I don't defend him because he doesn't need any defense."

Newton is one of the very few fortunate individuals who have played or worked for two of the biggest names in college sports history — Paul "Bear" Bryant and Adolph Rupp. And Newton, a two-sport athlete at Kentucky, got to know both of them well after crossing paths many times.

While Bryant coached football at Kentucky, he faithfully supported the school's athletic program. He followed Newton and other athletes by attending many of their games in baseball and basketball.

"He was a great baseball fan," Newton said of Bryant. "He would come to most of the games and even traveled with us when we played for the conference championship at Alabama (in 1950 when the Crimson Tide beat Kentucky in the playoffs). He went with the team and one of his assistants, Frank Moseley, was our baseball coach.

"I used to watch a lot of football. Football and basketball (players) were very close. We all dressed in this building (Memorial Coliseum). The football locker rooms were here and the practice field was right across the street. We practiced basketball here. So I got to know him."

Actually, it was 1964 when Newton first became more acquainted with the Bear in Tuscaloosa. Newton took a leave of absence from Transylvania for one year to work on his doctorate. He had been coaching at Transy for nine years.

"I really got to know him the year I worked on a doctorate down in Alabama," Newton said. "And (then-Crimson Tide basketball coach) Hayden Riley, Dr. (Frank) Rose and coach Bryant together made it possible for me to do that. I took a sabbatical at Transy and I had a teaching fellowship there. (I also served as) an athletic department graduate assistant where I coached the freshmen basketball team."

By the way, Rose was the president at Alabama at the time and had previously served in a similar capacity at Transy.

And four years later, when Newton left Transy to take the head coaching job at Alabama, Bryant became Newton's new immediate boss. The athletic director made it clear to Newton that he wanted a program that could win in the upper division of the 10-team SEC.

"I don't expect you to beat Kentucky and win conference championships," Bryant told Newton. "I don't expect that. I do expect us to be competitive and I expect us to do it right. If you don't, you're fired."

Newton recalled, "He was great to work for. He hired you, totally supported you and then got out of your way and let you do your job. He was there if you needed him, but he backed you.

"He was a good basketball fan. A lot of people didn't realize that. Some of the myths here (at Kentucky) about he and Rupp not liking each other, and him leaving because of basketball, and all that stuff, were not true. He was very supportive."

After the 1982 football season, the 69-year-old Bryant announced his retirement. Less than two months later, he died of a massive heart attack. Newton said he was fortunate that he and Bryant had enjoyed a nice conversation before the legendary coach passed away. Just like Newton did with Rupp and friends before they died.

"I went down to see him (Bryant) and spent the better part of an hour with him, not thinking that he was going to die," Newton said. "I've tried very hard to do this with people whom I most admire. (I don't) wait for the funeral. I go to see them before. I've been fortunate in doing that. I was able to do that with coach Rupp. I did it with (former assistant) coach Lancaster."

Meanwhile, Newton — who had Rupp's 6-7 grandson, Chip, on his Vanderbilt team in the late 1980s — was one of Rupp's favorite players.

"He was very good to me late in his life," Newton

said. "We had a good, close relationship all the way through to his death. I think I was probably one of his favorites in regard to the fact that I had coached and had some success."

After finishing his playing career at Kentucky, Newton continued to have some contact with Rupp. But the former player was still not very comfortable with the Baron, a perfectionist who could be overbearing at times. While at UK, the only conversations Newton had with Rupp was basically a "yes, sir" or "no, sir." Like most of his teammates, the player was intimidated by Rupp.

"I stayed afraid of him the whole time I was here," Newton said. "I kind of stood in awe and fear of coach Rupp. Some guys didn't. Some were able to bridge that. I just never was able to. I think I wanted to please him too badly.

"Then I spent some time scouting for him when I was coaching at Transy. I'd come to the practices and those type of things, and then I got to where I lost some of my fear of him. But we really never got past the player-coach relationship."

Born on Feb. 2, 1930 in Rockwood, Tenn., Newton came from a middle-class family. The family moved to Florida from the east Tennessee mountains when he was nine months old. They settled in sunny Fort Lauderdale in south Florida where his dad, who only had a sixth-grade education, ran a "rooming house, a kind of house that catered to tourists in the winter," said the younger Newton. "My father was self-employed. He did several things."

Newton's mother came from a family who was better off financially than his father. She had a difficult childhood. "Mother was from a little bit more affluent background," he said. "But (she) had lost her mother at a very early age. She and her sisters took care of their father, who was my grandfather."

Later, when Newton was about 14 years old, his family moved to a nearby farm in the country away from the Atlantic coast.

"I had a good childhood," Newton recalled. "I had an older sister who died when I was 25. I have an older brother, whom I am very close to, and (we're) 18 months difference. He had a career in the Air Force, a West Point graduate. So we had a good time growing up.

"Later in life dad subdivided part of the farm. His financial situation improved after my brother and I left. He was a good businessman."

When Newton entered first grade, he met a friendly classmate. Her name was Evelyn Davis. They became close friends and eventually married in 1951.

"Evelyn and I grew up together," Newton said. "She left Fort Lauderdale when we were about in the fourth or fifth grade and came back when we were in junior high school, ninth grade probably. We finished high school together."

At Fort Lauderdale High School, which was the only high school in the area at that time, they both excelled in sports. While Newton starred in football, basketball and baseball, his girlfriend was a diving standout, a 1948 Olympic Trials participant who earned a diving scholarship at the nearby University of Miami (Florida). Evelyn, who was a Southern AAU diving champion, later coached the diving team at Vanderbilt when her husband directed the school's basketball squad.

After high school, the couple parted, going to the universities in different states. But they kept in touch and got engaged. "When I signed a baseball contract going into my senior year (at Kentucky), we got married," Newton said. Today, the couple has three grown children — son Martin and daughters Deborah and Tracy — and several grandchildren.

Newton's son, by the way, is scheduled to work for the UK Basketball Television Network as a color analyst during the 1995-96 campaign, replacing Bernadette Locke-Mattox who became the head coach of the UK women's basketball squad. Martin, who played basketball at Samford University in Birmingham, Alabama, in the early 1980s, had previously worked two years for the Western Kentucky University basketball network.

The elder Newton is also a charter member of the Fort Lauderdale Sports Hall of Fame, along with tennis great Chris Evert, golfer Julius Boros and the late Brian Piccolo.

According to Newton, his first major influence in athletics was Clois Caldwell, who was his mentor at Fort Lauderdale High. "He was a real role model for me," said the athletic director. "He was a great, great person and a heck of a coach."

When Caldwell passed away, Newton attended his funeral. "I did the eulogy at coach Caldwell's funeral," Newton said. "The family asked me to speak which was nice."

Before going to Kentucky in 1948 on a basketball scholarship, Newton had wanted to play for the Tennessee Volunteers. That was his life-long dream. His family was from Tennessee so it was natural for him to want to attend UT in Knoxville.

However, a sticky problem arose. Tennessee head coach Bob Neyland and his staff wanted Newton, a three-sport prep standout, to play football. He said no. He didn't want to play college football. But Kentucky was interested in him in a different sport. Rupp sent one of his former players, Buddy Parker, to Florida to see Newton.

"I wanted to play basketball and baseball in college," explained Newton, who was recruited by several major schools. "There were some who thought I had a future in professional baseball and basketball was a love of mine so I'd made that decision.

"Recruiting was so different then. You really didn't make college decisions until late in your senior year. You went and visited a school or two. I came to Kentucky to visit right after I graduated. I went with a good friend of mine, an older man who drove me up, and they were having the Olympic trials. I was able to work out with them and that was just an unbelievable experience.

"As a matter of fact, they had an exhibition game out on a field between the (Phillips) Oilers and Kentucky, which made up the bulk of the Olympic team. And I just fell in love with it. I knew that was where I wanted to go to school so I didn't even visit anywhere else or do anything. I just made plans to come right back here and go to school."

When Newton visited the UK campus, Rupp's Wildcats, whose starting lineup was popularly known as "Fabulous Five," were coming off a national championship season with a sparkling 36-3 record and they were preparing for the London Olympics. The exhibition game, played in Lexington on a portable floor outside under the bright lights, attracted a then-record crowd of 14,000, which was the largest gathering at the time to watch a basketball matchup in the South.

At UK, Newton roomed with the towering 7-0 Bill Spivey, who played prep basketball in Georgia. They came to Kentucky at the same time.

On the 1948-49 freshman squad, they teamed (along with Guy Strong, Bob Watson, Lucian Whitaker, Leonard Pearson, among others) to post a perfect 15-0 record under coach Harry Lancaster.

Later, Spivey — who died in May of 1995 in Costa Rica — became an All-American, and Newton played as a substitute, earning a letter on Kentucky's third NCAA championship team in 1951.

Newton — who was also a member of a social fraternity and played quarterback on its intramural football championship squad at UK — said that he and Spivey never did try to take an advantage of Rupp such as missing curfews or breaking team rules.

"Bill and none of us did at that point," he said. "Bill was highly motivated to be a player. We didn't miss curfews because you had to get up the next morning, go eat breakfast and go to school. Most of us had eight o'clock classes. That was just part of the routine. Bill was good about that and Bill wanted to be a great player. He worked very hard at it. We really didn't have anybody that did.

"One thing coach Rupp had was good discipline, and yet at the same time, he gave you some freedom. He treated us more like adults. He really did. He told us what he expected. But you knew that if you stepped over the line that there was going to be discipline. You knew that."

Rupp once got angry with Newton who had a horrible practice. He told the player to sit down.

"Newton, do you know what you remind me of?" asked a furious Rupp.

"No, sir."

"You remind me of a Shetland pony at a stud horse parade."

The players, who were standing by, heard the exchange and laughed. "I thought that has to be the ultimate putdown," said a hurt Newton, adding that he has a lot of good memories of Rupp and tries to block out the bad ones.

Would Rupp's discipline methods of the past work in today's sports environment? Newton thinks so even though the society has changed.

"I think he would have changed with (the times)," he said. "He was smart. He was a people person. I'm often asked about that with coach Rupp and coach Bryant because I had the opportunity to play for the winningest basketball coach in history and then to work with the winningest football coach in history for 12 years. Both of them could win today. There wouldn't be any question.

"They'd have to do some things differently, but adherence to the teaching of fundamentals, the understanding of how the game ought to be played, all the technical parts of it would be fine. They had great people skills so that would work out okay.

"I'm not sure you could be quite as intimidating, but the man (Rupp) had such charisma about him that there was some just natural intimidation. And the other thing you have to remember about him is he had Harry Lancaster. Harry was a very big part of that whole team.

"I thought Harry, when I first played for him as a freshman, was very intimidating and I thought he was probably the toughest, meanest guy in the world. He worked you hard. He was a no nonsense guy. He also had a temper.

"But there was something about coach Lancaster where you knew that if you really had a problem, you could go to him. Behind that real tough, aggressive and hard nose (exterior), there was a quality to him that you knew if there was really something you needed to talk to him about, you could do it. When I started thinking about wanting to get married, Harry's the guy I went and talked to about that. I talked with him for advice more than coach Rupp.

"I not only played basketball for him, but the one year (1951) he became our baseball coach, I played baseball. In his early baseball coaching career, he was not a very good baseball coach because he tried to coach baseball like he did basketball. If you made a mistake, he wanted to take you out. He matured into that and became a very good baseball coach. He'd been a very good player. But Harry was a unique person. I developed a very close relationship with him."

Besides being a Rupp assistant for 26 years, including all of Rupp's four NCAA championship teams, Lancaster coached baseball for 16 years. In his first nine years (including a one-year stint in 1947) as the Wildcats head baseball coach, Lancaster's teams struggled with a poor 59-105-2 record. However, beginning with the 1959 season, the Paris, Ky., native began to win on the diamond as Kentucky posted seven consecutive non-losing seasons. Lancaster's best years in baseball, record-wise, were in 1959 and '60 with 18-8 records.

A standout baseball pitcher for the Wildcats, Newton signed with the New York Yankees in the spring of 1951, ending his playing career at Kentucky. He played in the Yankees organization for three and a half years. One of his better-known teammates was a future major league infielder by the name of Tony Kubek, who later became a well-known TV broadcaster. Like a typical minor leaguer, Newton looked forward to playing for the Yankees some day.

"I felt like I had a chance," said Newton, who continued to study at UK during the school year, earning his bachelor's degree in 1952. "It was so different then because you had 16 major league teams. This was way before you had the expansion teams. Class A and Class B baseball was very high level then as well as Double A and Triple A. When I realized that I really wasn't progressing, then I decided to quit. They talked to me about the possibility of me staying and looking at a career management. But I really thought (coaching in) college was where I wanted to be. I was coaching at Transy at the time and I knew that's what I wanted to do."

Newton said his two-year stint in the Air Force (1953 to '55) practically damaged his pro chances in baseball. "I was interrupted by two years in the Air Force, which hurt me from a professional standpoint because I came out at a (young) age and also because I had to make a career decision whether to continue with baseball or be a basketball coach. I had reached that point where I could no longer do both."

In the fall of 1951, even while he was in the Yankees farm system, Newton became the head basketball coach at Transylvania at the age of 21. His biographical sketch in various media guides will show that 1955-56 campaign was his first year as the Transy coach. But it was in 1951 when Newton actually launched his long coaching tenure before spending his time in the Air Force, where he was an officer and even played on the Andrews Air Force Base World-Wide Service championship squad.

On his 1951 appointment as a part-time coach at Transy, Newton said, "What happened was (ex-UK player) Walt Hirsch had accepted the job and actually had started practice. He had been in practice for two days and the (college basketball) scandal broke. With that, Walt lost the job there and Transy was without a coach.

"(Transy athletic director Harry) Stephenson called coach Rupp to recommend somebody and he recommended me. So I went over and took it on a part-time basis. It was not a good job at that time. They had no scholarships. They hadn't beaten anybody for a couple of years. But I got started and then after the service, I went on a full-time basis."

Rupp once commented, "I sent them Newton because he was the best man I knew for the job."

"I'm sure I couldn't have gotten the job without his recommendation," said a grateful Newton, who finished his 12-year stay at Transy with a respectable 169-137 record.

Early in his SEC coaching career, one of Newton's rivals was flamboyant Ray Mears of Tennessee. Mears coached at UT from 1962 to '77, compiling an overall mark of 278-112.

Newton thought Mears — who had coached at tiny Wittenberg College in Springfield, Ohio, before taking the job at Tennessee — was the most colorful character in the SEC other than Rupp. He was a master showman who entertained the fans with his team's fancy warmup drills. He was good copy for sportswriters. He gave them good quotes. "Ray was a unique guy," he said. "We had a lot of battles."

They knew each other for a long time, before entering big-time college basketball ranks. In the late 1950s and early 1960s, they faced each other as rival coaches of small colleges. But they were not close.

"Ray and I go back to when I was at Transylvania," Newton said. "We had battles then and it ended up in confrontations and we'd end up like this (at the sound of smacking hands). It takes a lot for me to do so, but Ray could just spark that."

While at Wittenberg, Mears had success with his slow-down offense and tough 1-3-1 zone defense as he won an unbelievable 121 games in 144 tries during his six-year tenure. He led the school to the NCAA college division championship in 1961.

During a six-year stretch in the 1970s, Newton's Alabama club and Tennessee continuously battled for the conference championship. The Crimson Tide had stars Leon Douglas and Charles Cleveland, while the Vols countered with the famous "Bernie and Ernie" show of Bernard King and Ernie Grunfeld.

"It wasn't Kentucky and the rest of the league," Newton said. "It was Alabama and Tennessee which fought for the championship. We had some very competitive times. He (Mears) would go right to the edge. He did it differently, but he was a heck of a coach."

Then in 1977, Mears had to quit coaching due to a serious health problem. The man in the orange blazer had broken down again and suffered manic depression. For many years, while coaching, he also had a nervous disorder, but was basically under control with therapy, including shock treatments, among other things.

As Mears recovered from his illness, taking medication, he became active in athletics again. He went to Tennessee-Martin as the school's athletic director in 1980. Eventually, Newton and Mears became friends and kept in touch.

"After his illness, we really got to be very close," said the Wildcat athletic director who has invited him to Lexington a few times recently. "We had a good relationship. He's an interesting man."

Now retired, Mears lives in Tellico Village, a small lakefront community near Knoxville.

"I saw Ray Mears at the SEC (tournament) and he looks great," said ex-UK cager Jim Andrews, who was heavily recruited by Mears while in high school. "In fact, he had some problems with depression and he just found out that all the years (while at UT) he was treated for depression, he was on the wrong medication. He talked about pursuing some sort of libel lawsuit because his coaching career ended prematurely. He had at least another 20 years of coaching.

"I have never heard him criticize Kentucky. He just wanted to find a way to beat them."

When he accepted the Vanderbilt job in 1981, Newton said he wasn't bored with the SEC job he held for only one year, serving as an assistant commissioner under the administration of SEC Commissioner Dr. H. Boyd McWhorter. Then-Vanderbilt athletic director Roy Kramer, who ironically is now the SEC commissioner, had asked Newton to take the coaching post at the academic-oriented Nashville school. Coach Richard Schmidt had resigned after two years at Vandy.

"I loved the SEC job," said Newton, who later interviewed for the league's top post in 1986 which went to Dr. Harvey Schiller after McWhorter retired. "I was kind of groomed to be the next commissioner, supposedly, and working with Dr. McWhorter was a tremendous experience. Vandy presented a unique challenge at that time because people had the attitude that if you were going to win, you had to sacrifice academics. I believe very strongly that you don't have to sacrifice academics to have championship teams in any sport.

"And everybody was talking about how tough it was (to win) at Vandy and, poor old Vandy, the academics were too tough in the league, while people were going the other way. I mean they were taking guys who couldn't read and write at some of our schools.

"That challenge was something that I wanted to do and coupled with the fact that Roy offered me such a good contract that I didn't know you could make so much money coaching basketball. I had never made any. I told him I wouldn't have gone back in (coaching) for the money, but I sure as heck wouldn't have gone back without it."

Newton's new five-year contract at Vanderbilt reportedly called for an estimated $70,000 a year, but he stated that the figures were too high. The new coach, by the way, did not get out of the administrative work he had enjoyed at the SEC office as Kramer also gave Newton additional responsibilities as the associate athletic director at Vandy.

"That experience turned out to be a great one for me," Newton said. "We were able to take a really once-proud program and do it right and solidify that 'you can do it' (theory). I still consider us as being a conference champion the year that they screwed us out with that tennis ball incident. We really were able to get that program into the NCAA, into the final 16. I feel good about what we did at Vanderbilt. To me, Vanderbilt was a big Transylvania. It was a fun experience."

Newton's eight-year record at Vanderbilt was 129-115. He never won a single SEC title while at Vandy. His closest encounter with the league championship came in 1989, his last year with the Commodores, when his squad finished second in a tie with Alabama as the Florida

Gators captured their first-ever SEC regular-season basketball crown.

The tennis ball incident in the crucial Vanderbilt-Florida game at Nashville in January, which cost his team a league title, is one of the most disappointing moments of his career, according to Newton. Florida won the matchup 81-78 in overtime.

Leading by two points with two seconds left in regulation, Vandy, with possession of the ball, had the game won if the boisterous fans from the student section hadn't thrown tennis balls. They threw the balls at moody Dwayne Schintzius, the 7-2 Gator who had been involved in a bizarre tennis racket episode several months earlier. The unsportsmanlike conduct by the crowd resulted in a technical foul called by official John Clougherty and Schintzius hit two shots from the line, forcing the contest into the extra period. After the game, coach Norm Sloan of Florida came away a happy man, while a fuming Newton blew his steam.

And today Newton is still bitter. He hasn't forgotten the ugly incident. "(That) damned tennis ball incident cost us the conference championship," he commented. "We've got the game won and some yokels throw tennis balls out there. The official overreacts and calls a technical foul on the crowd. It was just devastating to all of us, because it's like I told the commissioner and others, Vanderbilt, at best, might win the championship every 20 or 25 years. And here we are, we're going to win it. Instead, we end up at 12-6 and Florida ends up winning. That was a very tough thing for our team. But the game's over."

While at Vanderbilt, Newton, with his strong ties in the Bluegrass state, recruited many Kentuckians to the Commodore program. His last Vanderbilt team, which posted a fine 19-14 mark, had five players from Kentucky — Derrick Wilcox, Barry Goheen, Scott Draud, Robbie Graham and Frank Kornet. Seniors Goheen and Kornet were named to the second-team All-SEC for 1989. He also had Kentuckians on his other Vandy squads — Brett

Burrow (son of former UK All-American Bob Burrow), Phil Cox, Chip Rupp, to name a few.

Being the top sports administrator at a major university isn't easy with today's gigantic budgetary matters. In the old days, the athletic directors did not possess a strong background in accounting, finance or even marketing. They didn't have an MBA degree. They were mostly former coaches who didn't have the multi-million dollar budgets or other important issues such as gender equity and marketing to deal with. But times have changed. College sports have become big business. The athletic directors are expected to manage their departments just like the chief executive officers (CEOs) run in their large firms.

"When I was in school, we didn't have a marketing director," said former Wildcat Jim Andrews, who played in the early 1970s. "We had a sports information director and a couple of assistants. Their job pretty much was to keep profiles and stats on the players. It's not what it is today.

"Now they (the administrators) are smart business people with MBAs. They know how to play politics. C. M. Newton is one of the few people to make the transition from the old-style coaching to athletic director."

And Newton is fortunate that he has an able and experienced assistant in Larry Ivy, the senior assistant athletic director with an MBA degree from Alabama. Ivy helps manage UK's athletic budget of approximately $23 million.

The Knoxville News-Sentinel in 1994 had a special look at athletic directorships and briefly profiled each of the SEC's 12 athletic directors, including Kentucky's Newton. The Knoxville newspaper was complimentary of Newton, who is nationally well-known for his leadership roles in basketball circles, but said he "doesn't take criticism well, from the media or fans."

While Newton, who is extremely popular with the fans, has restored UK to respectability in athletics, he has encountered some controversies at UK.

In 1989, Newton admitted he made an error in judgment when he tried to take away 56 choice basketball seats from the students to accommodate the big donors for the Memorial Coliseum renovation project. To raise money, the ticket committee had decided to give these lower-arena seats to the boosters. Newton changed his mind after the students and the *Kentucky Kernel*, the campus newspaper, cried foul.

In the spring of 1994, as the rumors on Pitino's leaving UK for the Los Angeles Lakers' coaching job continued to fly in the Bluegrass, Newton got irritated. (According to a published report, the Lakers supposedly offered Pitino a $21 million, five-year pact.) Newton became upset when some UK fans had told him that they got tired of the rumors and wished Pitino would leave.

Later in 1994, Newton had to deal with the ugly talk, beyond his control, about the UK logo that contained the Wildcat's tongue which resembled a male sex organ. UK eventually changed that part of its logo.

And when Bill Curry and his football Wildcats were about to complete the 1994 season with a disastrous 1-10 showing, Newton felt the heat for Curry's coaching performance. He was the one who hired Curry away from Alabama in 1990 after the league champion Crimson Tide had played in the Sugar Bowl a week earlier.

A determined Newton created a stir when he told the Louisville's *Courier-Journal* that Curry will stay on at UK through the 1998 campaign, when his contract expires. He reportedly commented that "it's stupid" for the Kentucky fans "to waste their energy (thinking otherwise)." If the fans couldn't support Curry, then they should find another school to cheer on, Newton stated.

In the summer of 1995, Newton, coach Rick Pitino and other UK officials had to deal with the controversy concerning the departure of assistant trainer JoAnn Hauser from the men's basketball squad. Hauser filed a sex discrimination lawsuit against Kentucky because she said she was demoted to the women's team. In an initial statement released by UK, the officials denied there was any wrongdoing in the sex discrimination case, saying they have treated Hauser fairly. A native of Cleveland, Ohio, Hauser came to UK in 1986 as a graduate assistant in the athletic department.

But don't get the idea that Newton, 65, doesn't enjoy his current job despite the daily demands placed on him. And he wants UK to be a model program patterned after such schools as Indiana and Duke whose competitive athletic programs focus on the concept of student-athlete, not athlete-student.

"Coming back here, as it turned out, has been a real blessing for me," he said. "It's been a fun thing to see this program come together. We've got a chance to really be the model (program). And now that I'm getting near retirement, there are still things I want to get done. I think one thing I really feel good about is that I've not lost my zest for what we're about. I still have a lot of energy."

Besides his UK post, Newton also serves as the president of USA Basketball, which is the country's governing body for international competition, and is active in other affairs such as membership in the NCAA Division I Basketball Committee. Among his several preparations for the 1996 Olympics in Atlanta, Newton oversaw the selection of Lenny Wilkens of NBA's Atlanta Hawks as the head coach of the USA basketball squad.

In 1995, *College Sports*, a monthly publication, ranked Newton as the 21st most influential person in college athletics in its second annual Top 50 poll. In the previous year of 1994, the magazine rated Newton at No. 25.

"I've been really blessed by some of the outside opportunities I've been given and some of the folks I've run into," Newton said. "How that expands your horizon! I would never have met a David Stern (NBA commissioner) or had the opportunity to be with Michael Jordan or people like that."

His involvement in international affairs has caused
Newton to be away from Lexington quite often. Because
of that, he didn't see Kentucky's dramatic comeback victory over LSU in February of 1994. Rick Pitino's Cats were
31 points behind in the early second half before UK rallied.

"I was in Norway at the time of the Winter
Olympics so I didn't get to see the game live," Newton
explained. "All I heard was the score. When I got back to
the United States and heard how the game was — it was
just unbelievable, they said.

"The first thing my wife and I did, we got (then-
assistant coach) Billy Donovan to get us a videotape of the
game and took it home. I watched the videotape.
Knowing that we were going to win the game, I still didn't
believe we won it as I watched the replay of it. I thought
the significant thing of that game was the fact that Rick
never let the players quit thinking that they could win and
they figured out a way to win."

In addition to sports, religion has played a mean-
ingful role in Newton's life, both as a child and an adult.
His faith is Presbyterian. While growing up in Florida, his
parents stressed the importance of going to church every
Sunday.

"I like to think that I'm a spiritual person maybe
more so than a religious person," Newton said, "but I have
been a deacon and an elder in the Presbyterian church.

"I grew up in a home where church attendance and
working in the church were part of the way you lived. I've
done that through most of my adult life. As I've gotten
older, I've taken a little bit more of a sabbatical from the
church. I don't teach Sunday School like I used to or get
into the men's clubs and that kind of stuff the way I once

did."

And when he retires, Newton and his wife plan to remain in Lexington. They want to follow UK football and basketball teams primarily during the school year before taking trips in the off-season.

"I'm going to do it backwards from what everybody else does," he said. "I want to stay here in the fall and winter. I want to be here during the football and basketball seasons and then I want to go bone fishing or go to the Bahamas or the (Florida) Keys in April, May and June. Traditionally, most (retired) people go to Florida or warmer weather (locations) in the winter, but I'm going to be right here. We might spend a little bit of time in North Carolina. Maybe Colorado. Evelyn likes the mountains."

14 Unforgettable Cat

JOHN PELPHREY

About two weeks after John Pelphrey became an assistant coach at Marshall University, he made his very first recruiting trip as a coach. He had a scary experience that he'd never forget. No, it had nothing to do with the players. It took place in the middle of April in 1994 when he went with newly-hired head coach Billy Donovan. They had left Huntington, West Virginia, around midnight, traveling toward Lexington on I-64 to visit a high school prospect the next day.

For about the first 15 or 20 minutes, "we're riding along, talking," Pelphrey said in an interview from his office on the Marshall campus. "Everything seems fine. Coach is probably running a little fast, probably about 70-75 miles an hour. He had a brand new Cadillac. We'd just passed a semi-truck that was on the right hand side of us. There was a Caravan — one of those Astro van vehicles — behind us and a family was in it.

"We came out of this lighted area into a dark area and there were three deer right across the road — one right in the middle, one right in our lane and one in the other lane. And coach ran right over it. Hit it dead center. And it kind of exploded and had blood all over the windshield. It was kind of scary."

The incident shook them up pretty good, especially

Donovan, who is a native of Rockville Centre in New York.

"I started laughing after I realized he was okay," said the former Wildcat standout. "Coach Donovan had never seen anything like that. Being from New York, he doesn't understand why animals would run across the road. So we tease him a lot right now about that, but that was pretty wild.

"And the guys started calling us, teasing us and leaving messages that the game warden was looking for us for killing deer, stuff like that. People around here got a big kick out of it."

Before coming to Marshall, Pelphrey had one year of coaching experience, serving as the "restricted earnings" assistant coach at Oklahoma State under Eddie Sutton. Because of his "restricted earnings" position (now ruled illegal by a federal judge in 1995), he was not allowed to recruit off campus. He also didn't earn more than the NCAA limit of $16,000.

Coming to Huntington was almost like a homecoming for Pelphrey and his wife, Tracy, who was his high school sweetheart. Huntington is only about an hour drive from their hometown, Paintsville, in the eastern Kentucky mountains. They now make their home about 12 miles from the Marshall campus in West Virginia.

"I was very excited because it was an opportunity to come home," Pelphrey said of the Marshall coaching job. "It's good for me and my wife both. It's a chance for me to be a full-time assistant coach which means I get to recruit, get out on the road and evaluate the players.

"It was the next logical step for me to becoming a head coach some day. And I got a chance to work with Billy again. That was definitely something that I was looking forward to."

Pelphrey and Donovan had already known each

other during their earlier days at UK. While Pelphrey played, Donovan served his coaching apprenticeship as an assistant under Rick Pitino.

Even ex-UK mentor Eddie Sutton, his boss at Oklahoma State, encouraged Pelphrey — who played under Sutton as well as Pitino at Kentucky — to take the Marshall job.

"He told me that he wouldn't let me leave Oklahoma State unless he thought we had a chance to win at the school that I would be going to," Pelphrey said. "He talked to coach Donovan and he said, 'You have my blessing or whatever and you guys will do well there. You'll win basketball games.' So he was very good and supportive about it."

A year later, Pelphrey was especially glad to see his former team, Oklahoma State, in the 1995 NCAA Final Four.

"I did get a chance to watch them (on TV) and I was very, very excited for coach Sutton and for Sean (Sutton) because they're special people to me," said Pelphrey. "The team probably had the least talent since he's been there at Oklahoma State, but he had two great players in Bryant Reeves and Randy Rutherford. He can really coach defense and he's marvelous on the sidelines. So it's turned into a very good season for those guys.

"Even though I'm not there (at Oklahoma State), I kind of feel a part (of its program), having spent a year there and working with those guys and knowing some of the things they had to do to get there."

But he was sorry to see the Wildcats eliminated from the NCAA tournament in a 74-61 loss to North Carolina in 1995. Pelphrey said Kentucky had the better team.

"If it was a series, I feel confident that Kentucky would win a series (against the Tar Heels), but this is not the NBA," he said. "I personally think that Kentucky had a better team than North Carolina. It just so happens that you lose one game in the NCAA tournament and you're out. North Carolina had a pretty good basketball team and they played extremely well in the second half (after leading 34-31 at the intermission)."

While he starred at Paintsville High School, Pelphrey, an outstanding student, was set to go to Vanderbilt where C. M. Newton was the head coach. Newton had recruited the player for over a year, only to find him going to Kentucky, a late entry in the recruiting sweepstakes.

Newton was obviously upset when he learned of Pelphrey's decision in a telephone conversation with the player. But the coach, being a former UK player, understood the situation. He knew that the Wildcats would be hard to beat in recruiting if and when they became involved. Pelphrey, who grew up in Kentucky, had life-long dreams of playing for the Wildcats.

"Yeah, he was a little upset," Pelphrey said. "He wasn't really mad at me. He was disappointed, but he understood. Coach Newton was very, very honest with me throughout the whole recruiting process. I was going to Vanderbilt had Kentucky not got back into the picture. Coach Newton once told me in my home with my parents that if I felt that strongly about Kentucky that I should think about walking on there without a scholarship. He had played there and he understood the whole deal. I think Deron (Feldhaus) once told him it's kind of hard to turn Kentucky down when they come calling."

Newton did recruit Feldhaus, then a 6-7 star at Mason County High who later played with Pelphrey at Kentucky. (Feldhaus' dad, Allen, played for UK's Adolph Rupp in the early 1960s.)

As a senior, Pelphrey earned "Mr. Basketball" honors in Kentucky after averaging 20.1 points and 10.5 rebounds in leading Paintsville High to the semifinals of the state tournament.

When the 6-7, 180-pound Pelphrey arrived at UK in 1987, he joined five other promising true freshmen — Feldhaus, LeRon Ellis, Eric Manuel, Sean Sutton and Johnathon Davis. The recruiting crop was labeled as one of the nation's best, according to various publications. Prep All-Americans Ellis and Manuel headlined the crop. The 6-11 Ellis was California's Player of the Year, while 6-6 Manuel received similar honors in his home state of Georgia. In addition, Kentucky had a second-year freshman by the name of Reggie Hanson, a 6-8 forward. He had to sit out the previous year after failing to meet the Prop 48 academic guidelines.

But the skinny Pelphrey did not play with the Wildcats during his first year at Kentucky. Coach Eddie Sutton decided to redshirt the Paintsville native (along with Feldhaus) for the 1987-88 season. UK had a veteran team with seniors Winston Bennett, Ed Davender, Richard Madison and Rob Lock along with super sophomore Rex Chapman. In other words, the team was loaded.

"Physically, I was not ready to play," Pelphrey explained. "The chances of me beating out some of those guys who were there was very, very small. If I were to receive any playing time, it would be a very small amount. At that time, you could have 15 scholarship players. There were a lot of very good players on that basketball team and I wasn't going to play.

"I also understood that I needed to get bigger and stronger and I would be much, much better in my fifth year as a college basketball player than I would be in my first. So it was very beneficial for me. I'm very glad I did it (redshirt)."

With Pelphrey watching from the bench, the sixth-ranked Wildcats finished their campaign with a fine 27-6 mark, including SEC regular season and tournament championships, and two NCAA tournament victories over

Southern and Maryland. But Kentucky's record was later changed to 25-5 because of the NCAA sanctions placed on the school in 1989.

The following season of 1988-89 — Pelphrey's second year at UK — saw the big nightmare at Kentucky. The NCAA investigated the school's basketball program for apparent rules violations. Led by 6-7 freshman Chris Mills and sophomore LeRon Ellis, the Wildcats, distracted by the whole ordeal, struggled and finished with a 13-19 mark.

"It was very, very hard because at that time you had to deal with the media for like 20 or 25 minutes (almost every day)," said Pelphrey, who played as a second-year freshman. "It seemed like something new was coming up every day. Different reporters would come and ask the same questions. So it was always on your mind. (We're) always going over the same old stuff. It was a big distraction for the players, the coaches and everybody involved.

"It was a tough year on all of us, probably the toughest thing I've ever had to go through. I thought it was a tribute to the coaching staff and to the players that we hung together and competed and tried to do as well as we could."

Pelphrey, who averaged only 1.7 points a game in limited action that season, pointed out that the inexperienced Wildcats could've done a lot better if they had one talented player back on the squad.

"Had we had a guy like Eric Manuel (who sat out the season due to alleged academic fraud) on that basketball team, we might have won more basketball games than we did," he said. "He was the only guy from the year before who had any experience. We lost 13 games that year that we led in the second half. So if you win half of those games, all of a sudden, you have a 20-win season and you only lose about eight or nine games. We were just that close to avoiding that whole thing when you consider everything that went on which was so negative."

But if there was one lesson learned from that dreadful season which would help Pelphrey and most of his teammates in their lives later on, it's the experience of handling adversity.

"I think everybody who went through it is a better person today because of it or because of the way they handled it, maybe with the exception of Eric Manuel," Pelphrey said. "I'm not sure that Eric was ever able to recover because he wasn't allowed to play NCAA basketball anymore. That was terrible.

"The guys didn't really point their fingers, saying this is not fair, this and that. They understood what was happening. They accepted it. They made the best they could out of a bad situation. I think it worked out well for everybody as time went on. It didn't really seem, at the time, that it would be okay, but it was tough for a long time."

In May 1989, the NCAA placed Kentucky on a three-year probation, which included a two-year ban on post-season tournament action and a one-year ban on live television. That was the lowest point of his UK career, Pelphrey said. He thought the penalties for various rules violations were rather severe.

"We didn't know what to think about the penalty, but it was, without question, the low point," Pelphrey said. "There were some severe penalities. Whether they were justified or not, I don't know. Later on, there were a lot of schools which got in trouble with the NCAA and some got either more severely punished for less things or had less penalties for severe or more serious allegations."

Pelphrey basically agrees that there were probably some politics among the NCAA to punish Kentucky more than the other universities.

"I think they definitely wanted to make an example out of Kentucky," he said, "and let people know that they were serious about what was going on and about doing the right things. Anytime the NCAA puts a school on probation, they want you to suffer. They want you to have four or five years of bad times and make you pay. And it really never happened (at Kentucky). We were very, very fortunate that we really didn't have but one year of pain to go through."

As Kentucky was placed on probation, several players were contemplating transferring. But not Pelphrey, who saw three of his teammates — Chris Mills, LeRon Ellis and Sean Sutton — leave the Wildcats in search of greener pastures. In addition, Manuel wasn't allowed to play at any NCAA institution because of academic fraud. (Manuel later transferred to Hiwassee College, a junior college located near Madisonville, Tennessee, and to Oklahoma City University, an NAIA member.)

"I never really did (think about leaving UK)," Pelphrey said. "Kentucky was always the place where I wanted to play. Growing up, I used to pretend I was Kyle Macy, grabbing my socks, dribbling three times and shooting those free throws like he did. We were just really concerned about getting Kentucky back to where it was when we got there. We didn't want to be remembered as the guys who played for Kentucky when Kentucky was bad. It meant a lot to us to stay and have things turn out the way they did."

Many Kentucky fans don't like Sutton, who announced his resignation from UK on national TV during the NCAA tournament in 1989. They blamed him for UK basketball program's rapid downfall. Pelphrey said he is not shocked that many of the Wildcat fans still have hard feelings toward Sutton.

"No, I'm not surprised because if you or I only knew what we read in the paper, then that's probably the way you would go towards," said Pelphrey, a close friend of the Sutton family. "But I've been fortunate enough to be on the inside and to get to know these people and to understand what they are truly all about. So people sometimes can pass judgment in from the outside and it's unfortunate. But that's human nature. That's a part of this (coaching) business. It's something that you come to understand and realize that you don't have a whole lot of control over."

Pelphrey was saddened to see Sutton's son, Sean, leave the team. He and the younger Sutton — who played at Lexington Henry Clay High — were (and are) good buddies. Their friendship goes back to their high school days.

"I would have liked for him to stay at Kentucky because he was a great friend of mine," Pelphrey said. "We're very, very close. We spent several years together. We've known each other for a long time. When we were juniors in high school, we knew each other. We have a great friendship.

"I certainly understood why he had to leave. What a lot of people don't understand is they (Sutton family) have a great love for Kentucky. They feel very fortunate to have been there and have been a part of it. They have no hard feelings toward the University of Kentucky. It's unfortunate that it had to end the way it did."

After sitting out the 1989-90 season as the result of his father's departure from Kentucky, Sean Sutton inquired about the possibility of playing for the Wildcats under coach Rick Pitino. But things didn't work out and Sean later went to Oklahoma State to play for his dad, who had been named the head coach of the Cowboys in April of 1990.

In the summer of 1994, Pelphrey and his wife took part in Sean's wedding in Oklahoma.

When Pelphrey actually met Pitino for the first time, the player wasn't sure if the new Wildcat coach knew him.

Said Pelphrey: "Coach Pitino came into the room and when I shook hands with him, I said, 'My name is John Pelphrey.' And he said, 'I know who you are. I've seen the media guide.'

"But I didn't know if he knew who I was. I wanted to make sure he knew what my name was. It was our first team meeting and we hadn't really talked to him all summer long. I guess he was busy getting things situated, recruiting and those types of things and I hadn't talked to him."

And Pitino, the so-called Italian Magician, immediately turned the program around through his positive motivation and hard work as he guided the 1989-90 Wildcats to a surprisingly 14-14 mark with only eight scholarship players. Pelphrey, as a sophomore, saw himself one of the team's key players, starting 26 out of 28 games and averaging 13 points and five rebounds. Also, he and Reggie Hanson led the team with 61 steals each.

Pelphrey himself was surprised that Kentucky was able to complete Pitino's first year at the Wildcat helm with a .500 mark. Like many UK fans, he expected a long winter.

"We were small, didn't have any depth, had very little experience from the year before and were pulling an unbelievable schedule," Pelphrey explained. "He (Pitino) basically inherited a group of backup players. In the beginning, we didn't really believe in what he was saying. I think we were a little skeptical. Then we actually got into it and saw the hard work paying off. As time went on, we gained more confidence in ourselves and more confidence in him. Our games improved and we became a pretty good basketball team."

Pelphrey, nicknamed "Pel," fondly remembers two of his best games in a Wildcat uniform. It came against Ole Miss and Louisville.

In UK's 95-85 victory over Mississippi at Oxford during his junior year, Pelphrey poured in 29 points, grabbed seven rebounds and had six assists. "That was the night the (Persian) Gulf War broke out," he recalled. "I made five or six straight three-point shots and we won that basketball game. That was very memorable because it was the same night that we (the U.S.-led allies) bombed Baghdad."

Another of Pelphrey's individual highlights took place during the 1991-92 campaign in a nationally-televised game at Rupp Arena.

"The other game that stands out a lot is the game against Louisville when I was a senior," commented Pelphrey, who hit a game-high 26 points, including four three-pointers in UK's 103-89 victory over Louisville. "That was on ESPN. I think they were undefeated (6-0) and both teams were highly-ranked. I scored 16 points in the first seven minutes of the game and I ended up with 26." UK sophomore Jamal Mashburn added 25 points in the victory over the Cardinals.

During his collegiate career, Pelphrey saw his basketball stock soar. He became quicker and began to fit in Pitino's fast-paced offensive attack. He continued to improve.

After a fine sophomore year, he averaged 14.4 points as a junior, sharing the team's top scoring honors with senior Reggie Hanson, in UK's 22-6 season in 1991. He also received All-SEC honors and the Wildcats, who were ineligible for SEC championship, had the best record in the league, finishing with a No. 9 national ranking.

In his senior year, Pelphrey hit a 12.5-point average, the second-highest on the team behind Mashburn's

21.3 points, in UK's exciting 29-7 season which ended with a heartbreaking loss to Duke.

The forward credits Pitino for his dramatic improvement on the hardwood floor. "He was solely responsible," Pelphrey said of the coach. "(It's) because of the attitude that he took. He didn't look at our team as what they can't do. He looked at us and said (to the observers), 'These guys are smart. They can shoot. They're good passers. They've got an unbelievable desire to win. And they are working extremely hard.' That's all we wanted (to hear). We wanted somebody to take an interest in us. With his individually structured program and the amount of time that the coaching staff was willing to put in with us, that's where we got better."

Pitino once said the well-mannered Pelphrey is the one guy he "wouldn't trade for any player in America."

Sometimes Pitino used thick-skinned Pelphrey to motivate the squad. For instance, after the orange-clad Volunteers had dominated error-prone Kentucky in the first half of a 1990 game at Rupp Arena, the angry coach yelled at one player at halftime, using a psychological ploy to fire up the team. Miraculously, Pitino's psychological move worked as it ignited Kentucky to a dramatic 95-83 victory over UT after being down by 15 points in the first half.

And it was Pelphrey whom Pitino blasted in the locker room even though the Wildcat forward had a decent first half. Actually, Pitino was upset with senior guard Derrick Miller, who had a subpar performance, as well as other players. He used Pelphrey, knowing the player can take verbal lashings from him. Miller, the team's leading scorer, was more sensitive.

But Pelphrey didn't really know exactly for sure what was happening. He had an idea, though.

"He got up after me pretty good," he said of Pitino. "He was getting on me for a lot of different things. He told me I was too slow. I couldn't play there and that If I didn't start doing some this and that I wasn't going to play the rest of the year.

"I didn't get shook up, but I understood that he was trying to get everybody else fired up, get them ready to play. I knew I'd had a pretty good first half. He knew that he could get on me when he couldn't get on other guys in certain situations. I have always responded pretty well to criticism. It didn't really hurt my feelings. I just went out and played."

In the comeback victory against Tennessee, Pelphrey finished with a near-perfect game — 21 points on a 7-of-10 shooting, five steals, eight rebounds and blocked five shots in 33 minutes of action. Miller, meanwhile, bounced back, gunning in a game-high 28 points after 11 first-half points.

Along with his senior teammates Sean Woods, Deron Feldhaus and Richie Farmer, Pelphrey played his last college game in the 1992 Kentucky-Duke thriller. The Wildcats lost that one in overtime, 104-103. A very tough setback for Pelphrey and the team.

"After the game that night, we went out and ate somewhere real, real late there in Philadelphia — me and a couple of the players," said Pelphrey, who had 16 points, including three three-point field goals, in the loss. "We didn't sleep at all. But it wasn't like when the morning came, that it was all over with. There wasn't anything I did after the game to help. It took me a year to get over it.

"I finally realize the reason it was so tough was because we only had one year to play in the NCAA tournament. It really meant a lot to us to try to win and do as well as we could. and to have it taken away and to have your career end on a (Christian Laettner) shot with that small amount of time on the clock was really devastating for us.

"For a long time, I didn't understand why it happened to us because I really thought all the guys — all the coaches and everybody involved — were truly committed to doing the right things. And to do the right things, good things happen to you.

"We really didn't lose that game. We just lost that play."

About a week after the Kentucky-Duke game, the four seniors received the highest roundball honor from UK — the retirement of their jerseys — at a special awards ceremony for the team at Rupp Arena before 12,000 fans. Beforehand, the shocked seniors had absolutely no idea about the school's surprise "retirement" party. No one knew it was going to happen with the exception of athletic director C. M. Newton, Pitino, as well as the personnel in the sports information department.

"We had no idea," commented Pelphrey, who earned his marketing degree in December of 1991. "It was truly unbelievable. We'd seen the routine that coach Newton goes through when he retires jerseys. He got out there and gave his little talk, and when he got to a certain point, we all of a sudden realized what was going on.

"Because I had looked up and there was four blue covers (on the rafters), I turned to Deron Feldhaus and I said, 'You got to look up behind us. They have retired our jerseys.' "

His close friend didn't believe it, saying, "No, they haven't."

"He wouldn't turn and look," Pelphrey said of Feldhaus, "and about that time, coach Newton made the announcement. But it really caught everybody by surprise."

But the UK officials, including the sports information people, had been a little concerned before the ceremony when Pelphrey showed up at Rupp Arena early to be a
guest of a local radio call-in show.

"Had I looked up where I was sitting (in the show),
I would have seen the banners covered up," Pelphrey said.
"They were really concerned that I might do that and kind
of ruin the surprise. But I never once looked up, I guess,
in the hour show when I was there before the ceremony
started."

On Newton, Pelphrey said, "He had a big part in
retiring our jerseys and I'll be forever grateful for that.
That was the greatest honor that I've ever had."

As the Kentucky's 1991-92 season ended, the emo-
tional squad, especially the Farmer-Feldhaus-Pelphrey-
Woods gang, became popularly labeled as "The
Unforgettables."

Following his graduation, Pelphrey married his
long-time girlfriend, Tracy, in a 1992 wedding at First
Baptist Church in Paintsville.

While Pelphrey was at UK, he and Tracy used to
spend a lot of time on the campus for a shoot-around practice. "Every Sunday we'd go to Memorial Coliseum and I'd
make her rebound my free throws," he smiled. "She
always wanted to get out there and shoot three-pointers.
I told her she was a much better rebounder and passer.

"She graduated from high school a year before I
did. She went to Transylvania, so she was already in
Lexington by the time I got there." Tracy received her
undergraduate degree at Transy and her masters at UK.

According to Pelphrey, his wife is now a substitute
teacher and a part-time worker at a small clothing store in
the Huntington-Ashland area. She works part-time

because "she doesn't want to miss any of the games (at Marshall)," said her husband.

Shortly after the wedding, Pelphrey played professional basketball in two European countries — France and Spain — in 1992 and '93. His bride also went with him overseas.

While in Europe, they experienced one form of cultural shock. One of Pelphrey's passion is pizza. On many occasions, he tried to have the pizza delivered to their temporary home. He didn't have much success. "A lot of places don't deliver pizzas overseas," he said. "It gets very hard (to have them delivered).

On staying in Europe, Pelphrey said, "It's a truly different way of life. We enjoyed it, but it's not America."

Pelphrey — who is named after Boston Celtic great John Havlicek — comes from a sports-oriented family. His younger brother is in the coaching profession. Jerry Pelphrey, who played at East Tennessee State, is an assistant coach at Milligan College, a NAIA Division II school in eastern Tennessee. And his dad, Jack, is a former prep coach who now teaches at Lawrence County High School.

His parents devoted much of their time to the Wildcats when Pelphrey was growing up. They were loyal fans of UK. And when their son wore the Wildcat uniform, they followed the team almost everywhere it played — home and away. Jacqui, his younger sister, even attends UK.

Asked if his brother, Jerry, ever thought about walking on at Kentucky several years ago, Pelphrey replied, "I don't think so. He got a scholarship and he was proud of that. It was good for him to go out on his own and establish his own identity and he'd get away from me a little bit."

While Pelphrey's dad teaches at another school, his

mother, Jennie, is a teacher at Paintsville High.

It was his mother who had wanted her oldest child to be a doctor or lawyer. So no one really encouraged Pelphrey to enter the coaching business. In fact, his mom is one of several folks who tried to discourage him from coaching. She wanted him to do something else.

"Coaching is kind of a pretty tough business," Pelphrey explained. "There's not a lot of job security sometimes, but it's something I always wanted to do. And it's what I want to do. I guess I was the guy who kind of pushed myself into this field."

On Dec. 27, 1994, when Kentucky hosted Marshall in a nonconference matchup, Pelphrey made his first appearance at Rupp Arena as an opponent. He had mixed emotions in coaching against his former school.

"It was different," he said. "Previously, I had gone in there wearing the Kentucky uniform. But, as a coach for the first time in Rupp Arena, I felt like I had no control and it was obvious in the score (as UK won 116-75). I understand now how come some teams did crazy things when they came here to play us because it (Rupp Arena) is very intimidating."

Billy Donovan — who was also coaching his first game against Pitino, his former boss at UK — and his assistants had hopes of playing a decent game against the powerful Wildcats. But it didn't turn out to be a very pleasant night. Kentucky handily destroyed the Thundering Herd. It was a complete blowout.

"We didn't expect to win," Pelphrey said. "We expected to play better than we did. I guess we were embarrassed that we didn't play better."

On the loss to UK, Pelphrey attempted to look at the game on the bright side. He pointed out LSU's embarrassing setback to the Wildcats in UK's 1994-95 regular season finale. In comparison, Marshall fared better than LSU — margin-wise — when Kentucky, with six of its players scoring in double figures, whipped the Tigers 127-80 in Lexington on national TV.

"They beat LSU worse than they beat us," Pelphrey said of the Wildcats. "They beat a lot of people bad this year."

By the way, Pelphrey helped Donovan post a respectable 18-9 record in their first year (1994-95) at the West Virginia school.

Pelphrey admits that he wouldn't mind coming back to UK in the future as an assistant coach or the head coach.

"To me, there is no better place in America than the University of Kentucky and I certainly think it's the pinnacle of college basketball in America today," he said. "It has been for a long, long time. It's my alma mater and it will always be very close and dear to me. So if I was to find my way back there someday, that would be fine."